CRIMINAL INJUSTICE

America's Hall of Shame

BY

Patrick Mansell

CRIMINAL INJUSTICE
America's Hall of Shame

BY

PATRICK MANSELL

Copyright© 2018 by Patrick Mansell

ISBN 97809898738-2-6
Manufactured in the United States of America

Table of Contents
Criminal Injustice
America's Hall of Shame

Introduction

When the U.S. Constitution was written more than 200 years ago, there were three crimes in the federal code for which an individual could be charged: piracy, treason and counterfeiting. By the turn of the 21st century 27,000 pages of the federal criminal code cite 4,500 activities that can land an individual in federal prison.

Prior to 2010 there were 17,000 billing codes under which health services could be billed to federal medical programs such as Medicare and Medicaid. With the introduction of the Affordable Care Act, known as Obamacare, the number of billing codes has jumped to more than 100,000, making it nearly impossible for health care providers to comply with the law. Doctors and medical billing services are at risk daily of falsely billing the federal government – a crime punishable by loss of licenses, prison, and fines.

While intentional fraud is rampant in most government sponsored contracting programs, there are a great number of felons in federal prisons, charged and convicted of some sort of billing conspiracy, who had nothing to do with the crime for which they were charged, or any crime at all. Highly skilled individuals from business, science, medicine, law, and other professionals languish in federal prisons, stripped of their assets, their talents being wasted. Lesser talented individuals of the criminal justice system, prosecutors, investigators, judges and employees of the Bureau of Prisons step into the lives of these professionals and squander a lifetime of training and work that could otherwise be used for the betterment of mankind.

Corporations, politicians and lobbyists have hijacked the criminal justice system. A pharmacist or scientist who crosses big pharma can find the justice department on his back. The person who threatens a politician's chances of reelection, or gets sideways with an important campaign contributor, can be faced with a force beyond comprehension that will enter his life, and nothing will ever be the same again. Even in instances where the facts of the case have been argued in civil court and won, where an aggrieved party has agreed to a settlement and the books are closed, criminal charges can still be brought and a lengthy prison stay is a possibility.

Curiously, the government, legislative, judicial, and executive branches, all agree on the need for reform. For years the BOP (Bureau of Prisons) has butted heads with Congress. Legislators say they want to see reform. The BOP says it is stressed and needs reform. Presidents have all spoken of the need for reform.

And where reform has been implemented, where does it show up? In recent years the biggest breaks have gone to that class of felons that is most likely to re-offend: drug dealers, men and women the public does not want to see back on the street; people who poison society, endanger our children, and breed vertically integrated crime up and down the line. Admittedly sentencing guidelines for drug offenses have been draconian, and many drug dealers have received sentences far out of proportion to their crimes. Unfortunately, since the BOP, the guardians of society who warehouse these criminals, has no effective reentry programs to rehabilitate drug offenders, there is an 80% chance that they will re-offend and be back in prison within five years of their release. There are more inmates in prisons on account of drug offenses than for any other crime, and their recidivism rate is the highest of any class of felons.

Twenty seven percent of all U.S. citizens have gotten into trouble with the state or federal courts and have some kind of criminal records. More than two million men and women are incarcerated at any given time. More than 200,000 inmates are housed in federal prisons. Everyone at some time or other commits a crime. Some do it everyday; sometimes many times a day. The individual whose check is returned for lack of funds has committed a crime. The individual who even discusses a scheme to commit a crime has committed a crime. He is a conspirator.

There are felons who are convicted on the say so of another felon, someone who will give testimony, even false testimony, to better his own chances with the criminal justice system. Often individuals are convicted based on lies, greed, jealousy, revenge, or just plain cowardice. And the prosecutors and judges go along with it. With the cards so unfairly stacked against the defendant, no one is safe. No matter how well trained a person is to obey the laws, no matter how precise are the quality assurance procedures of an organization, no matter how hard an individual or organization strives to avoid breaking the law, odds are that some ambitious prosecutor can find a reason to investigate and bring charges. And with the justice department being so polluted by the influence of business, politicians, and powerful individuals, the average citizen doesn't have a chance. Every year individuals by the hundreds are dragged into this criminal justice vortex and subjected to inhumane punishment and unspeakable humiliation. Their lives are changed forever. They are stripped of their families, their assets and their dignity.

Preface

In the forty-six months in the Federal Prison Camp at Pensacola, Florida, where an average of 700 inmates are housed, the author came in contact with all manner of convicted felons. Nearly all of the inmates were non-violent offenders, worthy of enough trust that they could be allowed to roam free within the camp, and do work projects on and off the prison grounds, as they await their release dates. With the amount of diversity within this community, diverse in race, backgrounds, religion, and of course, the full spectrum of felonious behavior, the opportunities to hear fantastic stories are never-ending. Many inmates want to talk about what happened to them that ended with incarceration. Some fully admit the mistakes they made. Others exaggerate their offenses in order to appear more clever or adventurous than they actually are. Another group simply lies about the trouble in order to appear innocent when in fact they are not. But there is one group of inmates who I believe truly are victims of the system.

In the federal criminal justice system the prosecutors are successful more than 95% of the time. The largest percentage of convictions comes in the form of plea bargains, that is, cases that are negotiated and never come to trial. An attorney knowledgeable in how the federal prosecutorial process works will, under most circumstances, recommend that his client try to negotiate with prosecutors.

In the 1963 case of Brady vs. Maryland, the courts established what is known as Brady material, that is, information or evidence that is favorable to a criminal defendant's case. Failure by the prosecution to disclose

Brady materials violates the defendant's right to due process. Many rules of procedure were broken by prosecutors and investigators in the following cases. False testimony was admitted into the record. Threats against friends and family members were made, and favorable deals were structured for informants who gave less than reliable testimony. Brady materials were withheld in many instances.

A big topic of conversation in the American Bar Association, as well as state bars, is the question of prosecutors and their witnesses perjuring themselves. It is not unusual for a federal prosecutor to lie to the court, or just as likely, allow or encourage a witness for the prosecution to fabricate or exaggerate a story in support of a case against the defense. While there is no immunity for lying to the court for the benefit of the prosecution, it is rarely challenged and almost never prosecuted or sanctioned. The cards are often stacked against the defense, resulting in a conviction where no laws have been broken. The American Bar Association has this kind of behavior in its sights and aims to curb it.

The pervasive attitude in many federal courts is that the defendant must prove his innocence. The adage that an individual is innocent until proven guilty sounds good, but in reality is often ignored by judges and juries. When prosecutors and their witnesses present false evidence and testimony, the defense is at a serious disadvantage. Many more federal judges come from the prosecution ranks as opposed to the defense ranks, and the sentiment in the courtroom tends to lean toward the prosecution. Armed with the ability to make very favorable deals, a pro-prosecution attitude in court, and unlimited funding to carry out the prosecution, the U.S. Attorneys have all the ammunition they need to win nearly every case.

Another weapon in the prosecution arsenal is the theory of conspiracy. An individual does not have to be anywhere near the scene of the crime, and need not have taken an active role in the crime, to be charged as a conspirator or co-conspirator. Simply being a party to a transaction that had an illegal element to it can land an individual in hot water. Take as an example the sale of a piece of real estate. In such a transaction there are a number of participants: buyer, seller, escrow agent, title agent, lender, insurance agent, realtor, inspectors, and appraisers. If the buyer falsified the loan application to qualify for financing, a law has been broken. The prosecution can call this transaction a conspiracy to commit mortgage fraud and charge the buyer, seller, lender, realtor, and other participants, in spite of the fact that most of the people so named had no knowledge of, or part in, the transaction dealing with the loan. In another example of prosecutorial abuse, a scrap metal dealer buys and sells fifty tons of scrap everyday. His machinery operates for three shifts with welders and crushers, forklifts and semis buzzing around the facility all day and night. An ambitious FBI agent learns that in this massive movement of men, machines and money, over the course of a month the scrap yard has unknowingly purchased and re-sold five dozen stolen catalytic converters. (He found this out because he has already arrested the seller of the converters and that person composed a story implicating the scrap yard owner in order to lessen his own penalties.) The owner of the yard is indicted on a charge of conspiracy to trade in stolen merchandise. Because he paid for the scrap with cash he is also charged with conspiracy to commit money laundering. Not only is the owner of the yard charged, but so is his wife because she is the company bookkeeper. They each face twelve years in federal prison. In a plea deal the owner agrees to a four-year sentence. His wife gets two years, and the company is made to pay $1,200,000 in restitution, thus fattening the coffers of the U.S. government. As the expression goes, "You can't make this stuff up."

Black's Law Dictionary defines 'mens rea' as "the state of mind that the prosecution, to secure a conviction, must prove that a defendant had when committing a crime; criminal intent, or recklessness." Frequently defense attorneys will argue that mens rea was not present in their clients when a crime was committed. Not only is this argument ignored or overruled by the court at trial, but it is also equally neglected in the appeals process. And, of course, it is of no issue at all in a plea bargain situation.

For defendants who swear by their innocence, or who are urged by their attorneys to go to trial, another surprise awaits them. The jury process is archaic and deeply flawed in many ways. It is perfectly described by William Landay in his best selling novel, *Defending Jacob*: "They had nothing in common except their glaring lack of qualifications for the job. It was almost comical how ignorant they were of the law, of how trials work, even in this case, which had been splashed all over the newspapers and evening news. They were chosen for their perfect ignorance of these things. That is how the system works. In the end, the lawyers and judges happily step aside and hand the entire process over to a dozen complete amateurs. It would be funny if it were not so perverse."

The following stories are taken from personal interviews between the author and the subjects. Each story is a result of dozens of personal interviews. They have been written, edited and re-written under the supervision of each of the subjects. At all times it was understood that these are the inmates' own words without exaggeration or further interpretation on the part of the author. Further, during the process of interviewing these inmates, the author had every reason to believe them to be true. These men appeared credible and sincere. It was a job to sift through the dozens of inmate stories and settle on only the ones where the characters were believable, and the stories of their arrests or prosecutions showed egregious or illegal behavior on the part of the government. On the other hand, some of the characters are guilty of a crime. It may be the crime for which they were prosecuted, a greater crime, or a lesser crime. These cases have been selected to shine light on that behavior that took place in the investigation, prosecution or trials; where the boundaries of the legal process were ignored, stretched or broken; where witnesses were given the proper motivation to give false testimony; where politics meant more than the constitutional rights of the defendants; or where the courts misused their powers either by fiat or design.

Many of the investigators, prosecutors, police officers, and judges still work in the criminal justice system. Further, no proof has been given that any co-conspirators actually participated in the crimes described. Therefore, the names of some of the characters have been changed so that their identities cannot be recognized, using the same reasoning that they too are innocent unless and until proven guilty.

Criminal Injustice in the Rural South
The Ken Beverly Story

"Injustice anywhere is a threat to justice everywhere." These famous words, uttered by the Reverend Doctor Martin Luther King, Jr. are as true today as they ever were during the battle for civil rights. What can be said about our justice system when the federal government permits its prosecutors and judges to rely on what they know to be false accusations and testimony from unreliable sources known to have self-serving agendas, while disallowing evidence that can clear a good man's name? This is the story of a good man who did remarkable things in his life, saved thousands of lives, and provided treatment to hundreds of thousands of sick, poor, and elderly patients. This man helped build one of the most successful health care organizations in the nation, and was later framed and railroaded by an overly ambitious prosecutor and jealous and frightened colleagues. This is the story of Ken Beverly.

Ken was a native of Thomasville, Georgia. His family settled in the area in the early 1800s. Upon graduation from the University of Georgia in 1966 with a degree in business administration, he voluntarily joined the Army and accepted a commission as a second lieutenant. The Army sent Ken for training as a combat medic. Upon completion of that training, Ken volunteered for duty in Vietnam and was ordered to the 11th Armored Cavalry Regimen, the Black Horse Unit, in Xuan Loc, Vietnam. As an administrator and medic in a front line surgical hospital (MASH), Ken treated hundreds of injured soldiers and civilians. It was gut wrenching, but it was rewarding work. He helped to save a great many lives, but he also had to attend to too many wounded victims who could not be saved. He was one of those returning heroes who saw the worst side of the war in Vietnam, and brought home the psychic scars that accompany that kind of experience. Upon his return stateside, the Army sent Ken to Baylor University where he earned an MBA degree in hospital administration.

In the charming rural town of Thomasville, the Archbold Medical Center was a big fish in a small pond. Founded in 1925 by John F. Archbold, in tribute to his father, John D. Archbold, one of the founders of Standard Oil, the hospital was designed by northern architects and constructed according to the strict building standards of New York City. The Center was conceived as one of the most technologically advanced facilities of this type in the country, and is still considered one of the finest hospitals south of Atlanta.

John F. Archbold believed that health care should be available to everyone regardless of his ability to pay, and regardless of his race. In the segregated South of the early 1900s such progressive thinking was unheard of. As a magnet for indigent patients, the hospital struggled to meet its operating expenses. Established as a model for non-profit health care facilities, in earlier times it never would have survived had it not been for contributions from philanthropic families with names such as DuPont, Chubb, Whitney, Hanna (of the mega 3M Company), Ford, and of course, Archbold.

After resigning his captaincy from the Army in 1973, Ken took a position in Archbold administration as Director of the Archbold Community Mental Health Center, a federally funded part of the hospital. As a native son of Thomasville, and with his background in trauma, and formal university training in hospital administration, this was a natural career choice.

Any community hospital relies on government funding to support operations and growth. Archbold was no different. Throughout its history it has accessed public funds through such programs as Hill Burton Hospital Construction, the Federal Community Mental Health Act, and federally supported state programs such as the Georgia Regional Medical Program. Hill Burton established the standard by which medical facilities qualify for most kinds of public assistance. Through implementation of the Act, most modern hospitals have received funding for construction, expansion, and operations. The Archbold Medical Centers were Hill Burton qualified, and have received millions of dollars of government funding through this and other publicly administered programs.

The government subsidies provided through Medicare and Medicaid, beginning in the 1960s, were a lifeline to medical providers that treated elderly and indigent patients. A typical regional community hospital in any given year may receive ten percent of its revenue from private patients, approximately fifteen percent from commercial insurance such as Blue Cross and Humana, upwards of fifty-five percent from Medicare, and about twenty percent through the federal and state funded cooperative Medicaid program. Most health care providers could not survive without these two government programs, and millions of patients would be uncovered for treatment.

The federal government has vast amounts of money to allocate to regional and community medical facilities, but because of the huge sums of money available, and limited federal resources to monitor its use, the government relies on local governmental entities to put these funds to work under the supervision of state regulators. In order to qualify for state sponsored funding, a relationship needs to be established between the medical facility and the local hospital authority. In Thomasville that authority is the City of Thomasville Hospital Authority. The Board of the Hospital Authority is appointed by the City Council. These are voluntary positions that often consist of the City Mayor and members of the Board of Directors of the Hospital Authority itself. This interlocking directorate is structured to facilitate the affairs of the Authority.

In 1991, after seventeen years with the organization, Ken Beverly was named CEO of Archbold Medical Center. Growth and prosperity came to Archbold under Ken's leadership. "When I came to Archbold it was a hospital with fewer than 200 beds, with 400 employees and thirty physicians. We had to beg and borrow to make payroll," says Ken. "By the time I retired in 2008 it was a medical organization that boasted a 600 bed health care system that spread over five hospitals, four nursing homes, five dialysis centers, two home health agencies, a Level Two trauma center, and a world-class cancer center. We employed 2,900 people and had a medical staff of over 350 doctors. Our annual profit was $25 million on $600 million of revenue, and our development fund had $160 million in the bank. Archbold had become one of the most successful hospital organizations in the country."

So What Happened?

A series of events came together in a perfect storm that would result in Ken's eventual indictment. It began with an attempted takeover of Archbold's dialysis centers by one of its staff doctors, Mark Wood. Wood had put together a group of local investors with a plan to build dialysis centers in Archbold's market area. Having raided Archbold for much of its staff and many medical files and records, Wood's next move was to approach the hospital group about having it turn over its patients to his new organization. The Archbold board firmly opposed Wood's request, and the hospital was eventually served with an anti-trust action from Wood. Named as defendants in the suit were the medical center and hospital, Ken Beverly, some of the members of the Board of Directors, several doctors, and other individuals. The hospital spent a dozen years and $10 million fighting the suit, which was ultimately dismissed in favor of Ken and the other defendants.

But while the suit was in progress Dr. Wesley Simms, a co-defendant in the Wood suit, filed an open records request for documentation from the City of Thomasville Hospital Authority. Simms's discovery process in this civil matter uncovered discrepancies between the records he obtained from the Hospital Authority and those of the hospital itself. Those discrepancies centered on the minutes of the Thomasville Hospital Authority meetings, or more specifically, faked minutes of Authority meetings that never actually took place. It was learned that the Chief Financial Officer of Archbold, William Sellers, who had the dual responsibility as the registered agent for the Authority, had failed to call periodic meetings of the Board as required by its by-laws and state statutes. Instead of simply reporting this oversight to the Authority and state regulators, as would have been the prudent remedy, Sellers fabricated minutes for meetings that never took place, and placed them in the Authority's records. In Dr. Simms's extensive investigation this documentation anomaly was discovered. While the failure to conduct the requisite meetings could have, and should have been handled as a simple information transmittal to the relevant parties, this production of false documentation and the removal of records from the hospital raised questions about what Sellers had to hide, and grew into a full blown issue of fraud.

The audit requirements of the state auditors who administer and monitor the funding of certain federal programs require precision with respect to a participating hospital's record keeping. Billions of dollars are at stake and these hospitals are charged with the responsibility of complying with federal and state laws, and rules and regulations. In the normal course of a medical facility's billing of Medicaid, invoices are submitted periodically and are paid as presented. That is followed up by Medicaid making adjustments to the billing and deducting unauthorized payments, or overpayments, from future remittances. This simple routine goes on month after month and year after year. Archbold was no exception, and the responsibility for oversight of these payments within the medical group was with the CFO, Sellers. As the Simms legal team requested answers and documentation from Sellers, and the answers and documentation were not forthcoming, the investigation broadened. Sellers was caught removing records from hospital grounds thus exacerbating the problem.

The moment that Ken Beverly discovered the documentation discrepancy between the hospital records and those of the Authority, he knew there was a problem that must be addressed immediately. An emergency meeting of the Archbold executive committee was called. It was determined that this problem must be brought to the attention of state authorities without delay. William Sellers was dismissed from the hospital and given severance in accordance with his contract with the hospital. Attorneys for the hospital contacted state authorities and set a meeting to discuss the matter.

A new opportunity presented itself to Dr. Simms, and as the door opened, Simms stepped through it. If the hospital records and the records of the Authority were in conflict, then perhaps Archbold was not entitled to some of the federal funds it had received. Specifically, the hospital group qualified as a DISH facility. DISH stands for Disproportionate Share Hospital, meant that it treated a much higher percentage of indigent patients than other hospitals in the state. As a DISH hospital it was entitled to a slightly higher level of Medicaid funding for operating expenses. Archbold was number nine out of more than 150 hospitals in Georgia in the treatment of Medicaid patients. Qualifying for DISH funding placed a reporting burden on hospitals, but the two percent to three percent bonus funding was considered worth the administrative overhead as the additional funding could mean the difference between profitability and extinction.

When the Inspector General received the discrepancy report from Archbold's attorneys, its report to federal authorities caught the attention of the Justice Department. The United States Attorney's office commenced an investigation into the matter. Realizing that some funds may have to be returned to Medicaid, and triple damages maybe in order, Wesley Simms initiated a whistleblower action intended to benefit him financially from any recovery the government may receive. He pushed hard for the facts of the problem to be brought to light.

Several months following the disclosure of the false documentation and the opening of the investigation by the Justice Department, Ken Beverly's ten-year contract with the hospital expired. At sixty-two years of age he opted to take his retirement package. The ongoing investigation by both the Justice Department and the attorneys for Wesley Simms continued. It was not until more than two years later that Ken received a Target Letter from James Crane, the Assistant U.S. Attorney (AUSA) for the Middle District of Georgia.

This entire matter would never have happened had William Sellers not placed false documentation into the permanent records of the Thomasville Hospital Authority. But, as the investigations continued on two fronts, the aggressive demands from Simms for documentation, and now from the FBI on behalf of Justice, the heat was turned up. Local newspapers gave this front-page headlines for Ken alone on sixteen different occasions, another dozen or so on the Simms and Archbold investigation, more coverage than they had given any story since the bombing of Pearl Harbor. It was the story of the century in this rural Georgia community. Newspapers in Atlanta took note of it and covered it extensively, as did a number of business and medical journals. At stake was a claim against the hospital for what might have been about $4 million in Medicaid payments for the years for which Sellers presented false documentation. AUSA Crane saw it as a claim for as much as $14 million (triple damages), a criminal conviction, and as a potential opportunity to resurrect an otherwise mediocre career as a prosecutor. Not only did Crane want to recover those funds and the penalties that went along with them, but he also wanted to put a high profile player in the Archbold organization behind bars. Instead of going to the Hospital Board, or to Ken Beverly, for the information he would need to find the truth, he relied heavily on testimony from Sellers, the very person who created the problems, submitted the false documentation, and destroyed or otherwise absconded with hospital and Hospital Authority records.

Pressure was building from several sources. Wesley Simms was posturing for a whistleblower reward, and the civil suit from Wood had been pressing. But in a sealed settlement on the Wood suit just weeks before Ken's trial, no damages were awarded to Wood or Archbold. Archbold left Ken out of the Wood settlement. Of course, William Sellers was motivated to hit Ken hard in order to maintain his advantage with the Justice Department. Realizing that Sellers was setting him up to take responsibility for the false documentation and its ensuing problems, Ken launched a defense that included voluntarily submitting all documentation and evidence in the Hospital's possession to the investigators and proactively submitting to a polygraph test.

In its case against Ken, the Prosecutor claimed that, as CEO of Archbold, Ken had taken part in the scheme to defraud the government. Among the charges in the 2009 indictment was a count of conspiracy to commit Medicaid Fraud. The amount of the alleged fraud was $4 million. This amounted to approximately one quarter of one percent of the hospital's Medicaid billings, which by Generally Accepted Accounting Principals (GAAP) standards would constitute a rounding error. Certain of his innocence and eager to set the record straight, Ken willingly turned over any records the Feds asked for, and personally offered to assist in their investigation. Ken had spent his entire career building the company, and was well known in the industry as an honest, capable and respectable hospital administrator. He was not going to let what was testimony from the guilty party, Sellers, sully his reputation or damage the image of the hospital group.

This was uncharted territory for Ken. He had never before had to defend himself in a criminal matter, nor before the Wood case, a civil matter. In fact, in his wildest dreams he could not have considered that he would ever be named as a conspirator in a fraud case. In an effort to convince investigators they were on the wrong track, he pointed out that Archbold had a state or the art billing system with the Medicaid program. It had been billing Medicaid since 1966. It had gone through more than forty years of billing cycles. Routine adjustments to the accounts receivable were reconciled and posted every month. Annual audits were performed by Draffin and Tucker, a well-known and respected firm approved to perform hospital audits in accordance with government standards and corporate compliance programs. No major discrepancies were ever reported. Ken hired the most prestigious polygraph team in the country to test him. The results proved without a doubt that Ken's denials of responsibility and claim of innocence were irrefutable.

The Prosecutor's Advantage

Any criminal defense attorney will agree that the cards are stacked against the defendant in a federal criminal case. There are reasons why the U.S. Attorney's office rate of success in prosecuting crime is in the area of 95% nationwide. With unlimited financial resources, the U.S. Attorney's office has the ability to investigate and litigate against most defendants until they have no more resources with which to defend themselves. With this in mind, most attorneys will look for a plea agreement for their clients. While the plea will result in a conviction of the client, it will usually offer terms that are irresistible. An example may be the offer of a five-year prison sentence, three years of probation, and no fine in return for a guilty plea. The alternative threat could be to go to trial and face a fifteen-year sentence, a million dollar fine, and the implication of friends, family members, and co-workers. The risks of a trial are just too great. Couple that with prosecutorial misconduct and immunity for perjury, and the fact that the defense is not given the benefit or pre-trial discovery, it soon becomes apparent that the defendant is at a huge disadvantage. In the forward to the prominent defense attorney Harvey Silverglate's best selling book, Three Felonies a Day, How the Feds Target the Innocent, the famous criminal defense attorney Alan Dershowitz said, "Because federal criminal law carries such outrageously high sentences - often mandatory minimums - these prosecutorial threats are anything but illusory. They turn friends into enemies, family members into government witnesses, and employees into stool pigeons." In the text of that book Silverglate goes on to say, "Whole families have been devastated as have been myriad relationships and companies. Indeed, one of the most pernicious effects of the Justice Department's techniques - too often given warrant by the courts - is that they wreck important and socially beneficial relationships within civil society. Family members have been pitted against one another. Friends have been coerced into testifying against friends and former partners to save companies from obliteration, following scripts entirely at odds with the truth, and subject to the sole approval of federal prosecutors."

Ken's attorneys never made him aware of these risks. Convinced of his innocence, and desiring to clear his good name and protect Archbold's good reputation, he chose to fight the odds and go to court. This resulted in a two-year investigation where co-workers were given exhaustive interrogations by the FBI, as well as the veiled threat of prosecution, if the investigators did not like the answers they heard. It turned into an ugly and very public circus where some people who had been Ken's colleagues and friends for life were forced to turn against him. Harvey Silverglate, when describing the testimony of individuals who testify under the threat of prosecution, would say these people did not "sing": it was more like they "composed". Nobody was hurt more by this than Ken and his family and friends; and nobody benefitted more than William Sellers.

Ken was charged on a number of counts related to the submission of false minutes to the hospital authority, the documentation that had been prepared and submitted by Sellers, and submitting false documentation to Medicaid for the payments that were paid to the hospital during the years that those fabricated minutes were being used to qualify for DISH funding. There was never a question of whether the services for which Medicaid was billed were rendered. The recovery had only to do with the technicality of the submission of the made-up documentation. Ken Beverly denies having anything to do with that documentation; in fact he was not even a party to the fraud. William Sellers was the only one who had responsibility for that documentation. Under oath Sellers did not deny that he had caused that documentation to be used, but that he was certain that Ken Beverly would have agreed with his actions. He did not say that the documentation was prepared with Ken's guidance, supervision, or instruction.

The hospital hired Bruce Malloy to defend Ken, and paid his million and a half dollar fee for his defense. FBI questioning of hospital staff members had an intimidating effect. It had been well established that the hospital was going to give up Ken as the scapegoat in the case, and with the threat of additional indictments, Board Members and staff lined up against him. Malloy laid down a very weak defense and allowed testimony that was detrimental to his client to go unchallenged. He allowed the prosecutor to ask leading questions and often did not challenge that either. In reliance of Malloy's advice, Ken hired the country's most elite polygraph team in order to prove his innocence. What Malloy did not tell Ken was that federal courts do not allow polygraph results to be entered as a defense. (This policy confounded Ken and many other attorneys and defendants, as law enforcement routinely relies on polygraph results in its investigations.)

For his testimony against Ken, William Sellers was not charged with falsifying documentation or obstruction of justice. Instead AUSA Crane proffered a charge of removal of hospital property. He recommended no prison time or fine for Sellers because, as he told the judge, Sellers was the most cooperative witness he had ever encountered. Of course he was cooperative, he had an opportunity to lay his misdeeds off on Ken Beverly, and get away a free man. The statement that Sellers had no prior criminal record was challenged by the judge, himself, as his research showed that Sellers had a number of prior convictions. But none of this mattered. The prosecutor wanted to put the big fish away. In the hospital there were a number of individuals whose careers would advance with Ken out of the way. So the hospital distanced itself from him. And Sellers was out to save his own neck. In spite of the many instances of false testimony by Sellers and others, the ineffective defense on the part of Malloy, and the unmitigated dishonesty of several co-defendants, Ken was convicted in December 2010. Archbold immediately fired Malloy, whose failure to present an effective defense caused inestimable damage to Ken and to the hospital. Ken was sentenced on June 27, 2012 to two years in prison and ordered to pay a $50,000 fine. He reported to prison on August 22, 2012. A few days later the Archbold's management settled with the Justice Department for approximately $14,000,000. This settlement, as in the Woods case, was sealed.

The U.S. Constitution guarantees a speedy trial and justice. The minutes that Sellers falsified were from the 1990s. They were discovered in a 2005 civil suit and turned over to the federal government. Ken was indicted in April 2007 and tried in 2010. He was sentenced in June of 2012, and reported to prison in August of that year. He was released to home confinement in March of 2014. In spite of daily exercise while in prison, Ken's mental and physical health deteriorated during his incarceration. By the time of his release he was a profoundly depressed and broken man.

The Hard Fall of an Innocent Man
The Andy Bowdoin Story

Ponzi scheme. What does it mean? A Ponzi scheme, named after the famous swindler Charles Ponzi, is an illegitimate business model where the schemer pays high rates of return to early investors from the proceeds of the sale of shares to newer investors. Typically there are no real assets to back the investments from the new investors. However news of these high rates of return spreads fast, and attracting new investors becomes quite easy. With no real assets to produce earnings to pay the guaranteed high rate of return, the scheme is destined to collapse. Investors in Ponzi schemes do not know they are being misled. They are periodically shown impressive, but fictitious, charts and account statements that show how their accounts are growing, and their impressive rates of return. This usually keeps them from trying to withdraw their funds, so disintermediation is slow. For this reason Ponzi schemes can go on for a very long time. In the 21st century Bernie Madoff is perhaps the most famous Ponzi schemer, having duped the public out of as much as a fifty billion dollars. He was sent to prison for the rest of his life.

Well known to the public are the Secret Service functions of guarding the President and his family, and investigating crimes against the U.S. Treasury. Not so well known is its function of investigating financial crimes that are unique, that they cannot identify by name, or for which there is no precedent. It was the Secret Service that investigated Ad Surf Daily, Inc. and, for lack of a better term, or full understanding of the business model, called it a Ponzi scheme. The facts support a determination that no such scheme was employed in the structuring of the company. It was a clever business plan, and it earned a lot of money in a short time. It supported thousands of members, saving many from financial ruin, but it in no way fit the description of a Ponzi scheme.

Andy Bowdoin was an entrepreneur his whole life. Born in 1934 in the rural north Florida town of Perry, Andy was the son of a successful grocer and grew up in a middle class environment. In primary school he was above average in academics and played varsity football, basketball, and baseball. After a semester at Florida State University, Andy decided that college was not for him. His real desire was to get out and start earning a living. The initial investment in Andy came from his father who bought him a small piece of commercial property in the Perry area. On that land Andy built a commercial building in which he opened a dealership and service center for Mercury outboard motors. He also sold trailers and was a dealer for Glastron and Sports Craft boats. This business was aligned with Andy's love of fast boats, and he gained quite a reputation in boat racing circles. Mercury motors were known to be the highest revving and fastest outboards. His business thrived for about ten years, but in the recession of the late 1950s the pleasure boating industry suffered. Andy had to close the business and find another way to make a living.

Impressed with the motivational work of Dale Carnegie (How to Win Friends and Influence People), and Napoleon Hill (Think and Grow Rich), Andy started the National Success Institute (NSI). He purchased a franchise for the Napoleon Hill course and contracted with Dale Carnegie Courses to promote their classes. He owned and managed NSI for about five years. While Andy was building an impressive Rolodex of contacts through the years of promoting the motivational business, he also wanted to seek more and reach higher. He was also gaining a reputation for himself as a successful businessman. This attracted businessmen who wanted to share in his success.

Andy looked at a company with which he was familiar and wondered if it might be ripe for franchising. He approached the owners of 60 Minute Cleaners to see what the possibilities might be. 60 Minutes already had opened a number of locations throughout North Florida. Andy learned that a cleaning establishment could be opened quickly and inexpensively, so he devised a plan to attract investors each of whom would be a partial owner of a franchise. He would sell sixty limited partnership units for $1,000 each. The $60,000 investment was split: $45,000 for plant and equipment; $5,000 for initial operating expense; $10,000 for Andy's fee for structuring the deal, and he would retain a 50% ownership interest in the facility. By the time the business was fully mature Andy had opened 200 outlets and had earned several million dollars. Prior to embarking on the venture Andy, through his attorneys, had approached each of the states in which he intended to operate to make certain this ownership structure met their guidelines. He had assurances from each state that there was no prohibition against these limited partnerships. However, when the Tennessee State Department of Corporations looked closer at those partnerships, it decided that it did not like the ownership structures, and wanted the ownerships interests to be set up as corporations. With limitations of thirty-five shareholders in each entity, this was a problem. Each partnership already had sixty owners. Andy decided that the best course of action would be to sell his half interest in each of the facilities to the remaining partners. The unwinding of the partnerships was a monumental task, but was eventually completed to the satisfaction of the states and the investors.

Next Andy turned to technology manufacturing, starting out as a supplier of circuit boards for end users including NASA. This business morphed into a cell phone manufacturing facility with fifty cell phone retail outlets employing 250 salesmen throughout the South. At a time when cell phones were new and costing $3,000 per unit, the margins were quite agreeable. Andy and his army of salesmen were raking in huge profits from this new industry. But as time went on and the phones became smaller, cheaper and more plentiful, the margins thinned out, and the competition was fierce. Manufacturers such as Motorola and Nextel could deliver smaller, faster, and more versatile portables. The telecoms could supply minutes and bandwidth cheaply. Andy decided to move on.

Intrigued with Global Positioning System technology, Andy went into the business of manufacturing GPS tracking devices for automobiles. These units were purchased mainly by commercial users to track the movements of their fleets. This company was Andy's first use of the Internet to market a product. As he built the company, he intuitively perceived the value of traffic to his web site. With Search Engine Optimization (SEO) it became clear that each click of the mouse that directed buyers to his web site had value. Clicks meant money to Internet marketing companies. And with the great growth of Internet sales, Andy found a way to capitalize on this marketplace phenomenon.

In 2006 Andy founded Ad Surf Daily, Inc. While the concept was simple, the technology was not. Ad Surf was a web-based portal to thousands of member web sites. Other web marketers could register to be members of the Ad Surf group. Members had the privilege of being linked through Ad Surf to their own web sites. Through aggressive marketing, including rallies wherein potential customers could be educated on the Ad Surf program, Internet sales for members started to blossom. As the news spread of this clever marketing strategy, the public beat a path to Ad Surf's web site. As an incentive to bring in new members, Ad Surf offered bonus clicks or cash for recruiting new web site links. At the first weekend rally in Ackney, Iowa, 500 potential customers showed up. Two weeks later 1,000 attended.

Internet sales for members began to take off. All the members said that Ad Surf was the biggest reason their web sites and Internet sales programs were successful. Andy was working one hundred hours and adding six new staff members every week. The company had installed huge banks of servers in its Quincy, Florida, home office. It had a full time IT department, one hundred customer service reps, twenty-five people in the accounting department, and a sales and rally staff. As its popularity grew, the volume of members mushroomed. Within the first two years the company had signed 100,000 members. While the minimum fee for entry was $10.00 for ten clicks, the average member spent more like $15,000 for 15,000 clicks. Some members wanted to buy absurd numbers of clicks numbering in the hundreds of thousands of dollars. But Andy was not comfortable dealing at that level. He did on a few occasions allow members to exceed the 100,000-click threshold, but only on an exception basis. Money poured in like water from a fire hose.

The growth of Ad Surf never slowed down. Its IT department could barely keep up with the demand for data storage and bandwidth. While Andy never kidded himself that he could grow to the size of Google or Facebook, he also realized that the sky was the limit. As a start-up, a huge portion of that money was reinvested into the infrastructure of the company to accommodate its growth. But soon enough the profits mounted, and Andy and many of the Ad Surf members were becoming wealthy. Ad Surf had the kind of problem most people only dream of. So many people wanted its services that its customer service representatives could not process new applications in less than ten days. As its servers began to fill up, so did its bank accounts. In its second year Ad Surf was taking in millions of dollars every month. It distributed commissions to those members in the referral program, met its fiscal obligations with respect to office overhead, and was banking remarkable profits. In a single two-week period in early 2008 it took in $60 million. It was projecting a billion dollars a year in revenue within a year. Andy had become a wealthy and respected Internet entrepreneur.

On Friday, August 1, 2008, through the actions of the U.S. Government, the business, and all the dreams that accompanied it, came to a halt. Andy was out of town in business meetings when a call came in from the company Chief Financial Officer, Hayes Amos, with the alarming news that company payroll checks were bouncing. Perplexed by this foul-up, Andy instructed Mr. Amos to go down to the Quincy branch of Bank of America, where the company accounts were kept, to find out what was happening. There Mr. Amos was told that the Secret Service had confiscated all of Ad Surf's accounts containing $52 million in cash plus three CDs in the amount of $1 million each. Of the $55 million confiscated, $29 million belonged to members as commissions for the users they had brought in to Ad Surf. $26 million belonged to the company. Andy soon learned that the government had also shut down the Ad Surf web site.

Of this Andy says, "Can you imagine what this was like for me? I was already 74 years old when this happened. This was the culmination of my life's work and it ended all at once on that fateful day. My head was spinning; my body shook. I spent a sleepless weekend wondering what had happened and what would happen next. I'm surprised I lived through it."

At 7:00 a.m. on the following Monday, August 4th, Andy received some answers when a loud knock came at his door. When he opened the door he was greeted by ten Secret Service agents in their SWAT readiness uniforms, guns and all, armed with a warrant to search his house. Simultaneously a dozen like equipped agents were serving papers on his office for the same reason. But even with the drama of the storm troopers at his doors, they indicated that this was a civil case they were investigating.

Hopeful that he could get his web site back up and his people paid, Andy met with Ad Surf's corporate counsel, Robert Garner. Garner said that this matter, being of such huge proportions, and having been initiated at such a high level of government, it was recommended that Andy hire the prestigious Miami law firm of Ackerman, Senterfitt. Andy traveled to Miami to meet with the firm and was told that they would need a retainer of $600,000 to handle the case. It was Andy's best shot so he took it. He paid the retainer and the firm began studying the case. Attorney Jonathan Goodman called Judge Rosemary Collier (the venue was Washington, D.C.) and called for a hearing on the matter. The firm was asking that she order the Justice Department to release $2 million so Andy could pay his people and re-open the company before there was nothing left of it. On advice of Goodman, Andy did not attend the hearing. His absence angered Judge Collier and she ruled against the release of funds saying that it would be imprudent to continue funding a Ponzi scheme. In other words she had already pronounced Ad Surf guilty, three years before the trial. Andy feels certain that if he had attended the hearing, instead of listening to the attorneys and staying back, he would have received a different result.

Goodman worked the case for about three more months and asked for another $100,000 in retainer, which Andy paid. It was now nearly five months into the case and Ackerman Senterfitt had accomplished very little with the prosecution. After a particularly distressing conversation with Assistant U.S. Attorney (A.U.S.A.) William Cowden, the lead prosecutor on the case, Goodman notified Andy that he should be looking into hiring a criminal defense attorney as Cowden was about to go after him with criminal charges. Goodman recommended a criminal defense attorney from the Tallahassee area named Stephen Dobson III. At the same time he asked for another $95,000 in retainer. Andy contacted Dobson and paid his $50,000 retainer. He did not however pay Ackerman Senterfitt the additional retainer amount. He figured that after all this time, and $700,000 in legal fees, he had given the firm a fair chance to represent him.

Attorney Dodson traveled to Washington to meet with A.U.S.A. Cowden. He returned with discouraging news. The prosecutor said that he had spoken with Judge Collier and they were in agreement that a request for a sentence upon conviction of 40-50 years would be appropriate. Andy was being charged with creating a Ponzi scheme, money laundering, and wire fraud. But Dodson also said that with a plea he might be able to work out a 12-15 year sentence, and he strongly urged Andy to consider it.

The prosecutor gave Andy a proffer letter, known in legal circles as a Queen For a Day Letter. This letter opened the door for a conversation between the prosecution and the defendant wherein, if the prosecution believed Andy and thought that he was being open and forthcoming, might result in a better deal under a plea bargain. But with this proffer letter came a condition - before A.U.S.A. Cowden would come to Florida, Andy would have to sign over the assets the government had already seized and plead guilty to criminal charges. It was Dodson's recommendation that Andy comply, so he did. The property included the $55 million from the bank accounts, a lake house in Lake Talquin near Tallahassee, a condo in Myrtle Beach, S.C., and the four story office building in Quincy that Ad Surf had purchased, and was making ready to be the future headquarters.

In a three day interview with Dobson present William Cowden proved to be an arrogant bully. Dobson gave no objection to the demeanor or content of Cowden's questioning. After three days of withering questioning, bullying, and intimidating, the A.U.S.A. told Dobson "I want you to have that $200,000 in Garner's (corporate counsel to Ad Surf) legal trust fund. Call him right now and tell him to send that money. Use my cell phone." Andy looked in his address book, produced Garner's number, and gave it to Dobson. Dobson made the call and told Garner what he wanted. But Garner explained that half that money had already been spent on another legal matter, and only half remained in the account. Dobson told him to send that. Garner asked to speak to Andy to make certain he was in agreement. Andy told him that he was and to please go ahead and send the money. Then Cowden took the phone and informed Garner that if he did not immediately send those funds he would be charged with money laundering. Garner did as requested and sent the $100,000.

On his own that evening Andy got to thinking about the events of the day. He concluded that he had been victimized by Cowden and Dobson, and that the payment to Dobson was a payoff in exchange for Dobson convincing Andy to sign over the seized assets and plead guilty. The following morning Andy called Dobson and fired him with prejudice. He told Dobson to call Cowden and tell him that he was not going to sign the plea agreement and that he was going to fight the charges.

When Ad Surf collapsed, thousands of people who relied on the web site and business it provided were suddenly left with no source of income. Some were forced to declare bankruptcy. During this period Andy conducted conference calls with members several times a week. He received testimonials from scores of members that Ad Surf was their only source of income and that shutting it down would devastate them financially. But as time passed it became obvious that the government had no intention of allowing the web site to function, or to return the assets to their rightful owners. Several years later the justice department hired a third party to contact each member telling them that if they wanted a return of their advertising fees they were to send proof of payment and sign an affidavit that the money used to purchase Internet clicks was intended as an investment. Justice was trying to build a criminal case against Andy, and these affidavits were incriminating. They wanted to make the advertising fees look like investments so they could couch the business model as a Ponzi scheme. Of course, Cowden was promising money, so people were motivated. At one of his hearings in the criminal case Andy heard Cowden tell his attorney, "I have 15,000 signed affidavits that this is an investment." The justice department had bought these affidavits and sealed the case against Andy and Ad Surf using money it had confiscated form the defendants.

In his search to find a criminal defense attorney to replace Dobson, Andy came across Charles Murray of Bonita Springs, Florida. Murray was known for being the attorney who defended a single defendant in a fraud case involving a real estate investment trust and 300 other defendants. Murray's client was the only defendant to be acquitted. The other 300 defendants were convicted and sentenced. This, and other impressive credentials of Murray's, convinced Andy that this was the right attorney to take over his case. Murray hired the very talented Mike Mac Donald of Naples, Florida, as co-counsel.

When Andy explained how he had been shaken down by his previous attorney and Cowden, Murray placed a call to the prosecutor. He inquired as to the disposition of that $100,000 payment. Cowden stammered and said he would have to call Dobson to see if those funds had been forwarded to the Justice Department yet. Andy believes that Cowden and Dobson now realized that their ploy to defraud him had been exposed. Two weeks later William Cowden retired from the prosecutor's office. Dwight Switzer, a retired attorney, helped Andy draft a letter to Dobson explaining his position with respect to those funds. The letter threatened bar action and criminal charges if those funds were not returned immediately. Three days later Andy received a cashier's check from Dobson in the amount of $100,000. In Andy's mind this confirmed that Dobson, who was supposed to be representing him, had conspired with the U.S. Attorney to trick Andy into turning over the Ad Surf assets and plead guilty in exchange for a payoff of $100,000 to Dobson.

Because he lived in North Florida, and his new attorneys were from South Florida 300 miles away, and because they had to meet several times a week, Andy rented a home in the quiet, gated community of Englewood. One day while enjoying life in this peaceful place, eight Secret Service agents barged into the neighborhood in four SUVs with lights flashing. Naturally all of the neighbors showed up to see what was causing the commotion. The agents arrested Andy and marched him out in handcuffs and leg irons in front of the entire neighborhood. They drove Andy to the Federal Detention Center in Tampa, Florida.

A bond hearing was set for 6:30 that evening. Two prosecutors objected to the bond saying Andy had $8 million in offshore accounts and he was a flight risk. Judge Collier called from Washington and told the hearing judge the same thing. The judge recognized two Secret Service agents in the gallery and asked if they had any proof of that statement about offshore bank accounts. The agents ashamedly admitted that they did not. The judge's reaction was to say, "OK, let's talk about the bond," denying the prosecutors' objection. Andy's daughter-in-law, Judy Harris, attended the hearing and offered to sign a personal bond for Andy's release. Andy's wife put up the deed to her house and a small commercial building as collateral. The judge accepted, and Andy was released.

Attorney Murray was armed with two convincing pieces of evidence in support of his client. Prior to the raid on Andy's

Quincy house and the Ad Surf offices, Andy had commissioned a study of Ad Surf for a client who was considering making a large entry into the Ad Surf web site. This study was to come from a firm that specialized in litigating Ponzi cases. The firm was that same one who handled the famous Amway case and won it. Amway had been charged with operating a Ponzi scheme and was shut down for three years. After the firm studied Ad Surf, it produced a twenty-seven-page affidavit in which it concluded that Ad Surf was not a Ponzi scheme, and gave all the reasons why not. In the same time frame Andy hired Keith Laggos to do a study of Ad Surf's practices and business model. For twenty-five years Laggos had been the publisher of a multi-level marketing magazine and was considered the nations leading expert on the subject. His fourteen-page affidavit also concluded that Ad Surf was not a Ponzi scheme.

Murray was building a strong defense. He told the prosecutor that, in Andy's defense, he would be calling these two men as witnesses and entering the affidavits into evidence. Next Murray hired a jury consulting firm to see where they would stand should they decide to go to trial. The firm conducted interviews of people who may be typical of jurors. They conducted a mock trial to test the waters. Unfortunately for Andy, the results were not favorable. It was determined that the typical jury would not understand the evidence and could render an unfavorable verdict. Next Andy hired an accounting firm to perform an audit of Ad Surf's practices to see if that would make a difference. But Andy was running out of money and he had to put the audit on hold.

In order to get the auditors back to work Andy needed an income, so he started working for another network marketing company. This network already had 800,000 members and was very successful. Andy's idea was to solicit the 100,000 Ad Surf members to join this new network.

When he contacted them, he received enthusiastic support. But in Ad Surf's own network were several Secret Service agents. When solicited by Andy, they brought this fact to the authorities who in turn filed additional charges with the court. Out of all these hundreds of thousands of members, Andy was the only one charged. When Judge Collier heard of the new charges, knowing nothing at all about the company, she declared it a Ponzi scheme and had Andy arrested and locked up in the Federal Detention Center (FDC) in Washington, D.C.

Time marched on while Andy sat in a jail cell. Several weeks later was the hearing at which Andy pled guilty. Judge Collier accepted his plea and set a date for sentencing. But Andy was not released during the interval between the plea hearing and the sentencing, as is the usual procedure. The judge made him remain in the detention center until the sentencing date. Throughout this entire process the judge had shown a great deal of prejudice toward Andy. There was no way he was going to get a break from her. And so it was that Judge Collier sentenced this seventy-seven-year-old man to seventy-eight months in prison, the exact amount that had been spelled out in the plea. No restitution was ordered, which is typically the case when no victims have been injured. Andy spent the next two and a half months in the Washington, D.C. Federal Detention Center. From there he was shipped to the Warsaw, VA, FDC where he spent two months. From there he was transported to Oklahoma City on the Bureau of Prisons' airplane called "Con Air." He remembers spending two freezing weeks in Oklahoma wearing only a thin paper uniform in 50-degree temperatures, before being shipped to Jacksonville, FL, and then on to Tallahassee for the last leg of the trip. Two weeks later he boarded a prison bus bound for the Federal Prison Camp at Pensacola, FL. Throughout all these moves Andy was kept in handcuffs and ankle shackles.

The tragedy of federal prison confinement often has more to do with the human-interest side of the story than the felon or the victims. In Andy's case there were no victims, and the government confiscated a great deal of money that it never accounted for. But Andy has been a victim more than anyone. His company has been destroyed, as has his life's work. He has very few assets to rely upon if he lives to see the other side of the prison fence. His wife has stood by him, and his daughter-in-law, Judy Harris, and stepson, George Harris, have been a bright spot for him. His four other children have decided not to stay in touch with him. But many of the 100,000 Ad Surf members remain in contact with him, which gives him great strength. Life can sometimes be tough in prison. But when there is prosecutorial misconduct, and the justice system is biased, and family units break down, the hurt is many times worse.

The Pain of Treating Pain
The Dr. Gerard DiLeo Story

Dr. Lynn Webster, the president of the American Academy of Pain Medicine, tells the story of a patient of his who lived with debilitating pain following three back operations. Another procedure for this surgery-weary patient was out of the question and the only treatment indicated was to mask the pain. The highest form of pain treatment was used when a device was implanted into the patient's spinal canal for direct application of strong opioids. The device delivered medication directly to the source of the pain so Dr. Webster could wean the patient off his oral doses. It was the doctor's intention to gradually cut back on the dosages so that eventually he could level off at a sustainable rate and avoid a buildup of dangerous side effects and addiction to the medication. But each time Dr. Webster would manipulate the regimen the patient complained of unbearable pain. The distraught patient told the doctor he could not live like this. Dr. Webster, hoping more than knowing, would respond, "It will get better." The doctor knew he was walking the tight line between providing the patient with the relief he needed and over-prescribing scheduled medications. Cognizant of the potential legal ramifications of being accused of over-prescribing, the doctor gave care as he felt appropriate, but tried hard not to cross the line with too much pain medication. Sadly, the day came when the patient's daughter called to say that her father had died of a self-inflicted gunshot wound. He had left a note saying he couldn't live with the pain. He loved his daughter but felt he was of no value to her any longer. He couldn't see a future; he had no hope, no life. Dr. Webster was left asking himself if his concern for his own freedom and licensure had played a part in this tragedy.

Contrast this grim story with a statement from Dr. Celia Mouton, the chief of investigations for the Louisiana State Board of Medical Examiners (LSBME) in a conversation with Dr. Alan Dennis. Dr. Dennis was a member of a special committee on pain management chaired by Dr. Gerard DiLeo, a thirty-five-year veteran in obstetrics and gynecology, and innovator in pelvic pain management. Dr. Mouton stated, "There is no such thing as chronic pain." How absurd must a statement like this sound to a professional medical practitioner? It is doubtful that a single physician in the entire world would agree with such a statement. Few lay people would agree. But this is the kind of thinking that Dr. DiLeo faced as he tried to defend himself against criminal charges with Dr. Mouton as a witness for the prosecutor; a prosecutor who lied, presented false testimony and planted evidence in the case against him. His problems were further exacerbated by the fact that LSBME, as opposed to committing itself to a higher standard of medicine in the State of Louisiana, is focused only on catching and punishing medical practitioners who violate its vague and sketchy rules.

Dr. DiLeo attended LSU in Baton Rouge as an undergraduate and received his Bachelor of Arts degree in zoology in 1973. He attended LSU School of Medicine in New Orleans, and received his M.D. degree in 1977. In the period between 1977 and 1981 he took residency in obstetrics and gynecology at LSU Charity Hospital in New Orleans. He married his wife, Linda, in 1980. The DiLeos have five children, daughter Phoebe, a world ranked tennis player, sons Blaise and Evan both of whom attended the Air Force Academy in Colorado Springs, daughter Cara, and a special needs son named Luke. Luke had many permanent medical problems as a result of a twelve-week premature birth. An inter-cranial hemorrhage left him with heart and liver failure and many other health related issues. The DiLeos also fostered four other children, one of whom named Cara they adopted, and they raised three of their nieces. While Dr. DiLeo and Linda have always relished being the primary caregivers of their son, their daughters and other sons have cheerfully participated in Luke's care. It was a large and happy family.

For thirty-two years Dr. DiLeo owned and managed a successful OB/GYN practice, and in the period between 1998 and 2000 he was chief of staff at Lakeview Medical Center in Covington, LA. Throughout all his years in practice one of Dr. DiLeo's great frustrations was his medical specialty's inability to come up with an adequate solution for female pelvic pain. Pelvic pain in women can be caused by a number of reasons, but early childhood sexual abuse is very frequently the cause. The trauma of sexual abuse in women can cause them to have severely adverse reactions to anything related to sex. Sometimes just the event of a man coming in close contact can cause a reaction. The pelvic muscles can spasm involuntarily. Some women have this reaction one hundred times a day, and before long severe cramps develop and the pain can be excruciating. Desperate for relief, these victims try all kinds of pain remedies but usually to no avail. As doctors and friends begin to doubt a real problem exists, the patient can become frantic and even begin to believe the pain is all in her head. The problem grows, and the patient's physical and mental health can nosedive into something serious enough to foster thoughts of suicide. Often Dr. DiLeo would refer patients to pain specialists to ease their suffering. Too frequently these patients would be told the specialist had no solution short of treatment that would affect their entire bodies: oral opioids. Dr. DiLeo was looking for something more specific for his patients, but by joining the American Association of Pain Management, he could find no solution there either.

In 2000 Dr. DiLeo made some life altering changes. He received a deal with McGraw-Hill Publishing to write the book "The Anxious Parents' Guide to Pregnancy" which was published in 2002. In order to find time to write this book he had to cut back on his medical practice. He decided to stop practicing obstetrics and concentrate exclusively on gynecology. He took the two years to write his book, continued practicing medicine, and pursued expertise in pelvic pain.

In 2004, while still running his gynecology practice, Dr. DiLeo joined, on a part time basis, Global Pain Management, a network with offices in Metairie and Covington, LA. Here he could work in a place where he could continue his gynecology practice and hone his knowledge of pain management to a much higher degree. This exposure would place Dr. DiLeo in the unique position of being a board-certified OB/GYN in combination with a comprehensive grasp of pain management. A symbiotic relationship existed between Global and Dr. DiLeo. Global had a network of needy patients and the physical plant to treat them. Dr. DiLeo had the medical and scientific expertise to help make Global into a first-class pain management facility. Both Dr. DiLeo and Global were aware of the issues related to pain clinics and the over-prescribing of opioids. Pill mills were a large target for the justice system, and extreme care would have to be taken to screen patients and avoid conflicts with the law while advancing the science.

Before joining Global Dr. DiLeo used caution vetting the organization. One of the Clinics' owners was a former law enforcement officer. Everywhere he inquired he received excellent feedback. And so, Dr. DiLeo joined the staff of Global for the opportunity to become the consummate expert in his new chosen sub-specialty. It was Dr. DiLeo's place to develop protocols for Global that would ensure a quality control process that followed, or superseded the standards of LSBME and other regulatory agencies. Under his guidance

42

the clinics employed and trained first class medical practitioners. As such, through its comprehensive intake process, sixty percent of its prospective patients were rejected because they could not pass Global's rigid screening process. Dr. DiLeo hired Dr. Joe Pastorek as its adjunct medical director. Dr. Pastorek is man who is considered to have the mental capabilities of a genius, with medical and law degrees, and a Master's Degree in physics. He practiced at the LSU hospital and taught advanced studies in medicine at the LSU School of Medicine.

In an effort to be proactive with compliance laws and industry standards, Dr. DiLeo met with Sheriff Jack Strain of the St. Tammany Parrish Sheriff's Office. He proposed a summit meeting among law enforcement and practitioners within the pain management profession. In attendance at this meeting were psychiatrists, officials from law enforcement, addictionologists, anesthesiologists, and two DEA agents from Washington. Conspicuously absent from the meeting was Celia Mouton, or any other representative of LSBME, even though invitations were extended. This consortium, through this meeting and subsequent broadcast emails, created a twenty-six-page manifesto for standards of treatment for chronic pain. The LSBME could not be convinced to participate in adopting these standards, nor would it contribute its voice to this important project. In fact, Celia Mouton had been quoted as saying earlier in a conversation with Alan Dennis, "Just because you're following the rules doesn't mean you're not in trouble," further evidence of that agency's "gotcha" mentality with respect to regulating the medical profession in Louisiana.

From 2004 to 2006 Dr. DiLeo split his time between his gynecology practice and part time work for Global. When Hurricane Katrina hit the area in August of 2005 things changed dramatically. Dr. DiLeo's home was in a mandatory evacuation zone so the family was sent to Florida to find a safe place to ride it out. Dr. DiLeo stayed behind to tend to his patients. His home survived the storm and was converted into a shelter of sorts. In the ensuing weeks the home was a refuge for eighteen friends, relatives, and co-workers for a very long time. Soon it became obvious that living conditions in New Orleans would not be suitable for Luke, so the family established a permanent residence in Bradenton, Florida. Dr. DiLeo spit his time between these two areas, tending to patients during the week and the family on weekends.

It was during this time that the owner of Global, Dennis Caroni, noticed an opportunity for a clinic in the Florida panhandle. He decided to open a new clinic in Pensacola. Dr. DiLeo had no real involvement in the day-to-day operation of that facility, but it was opened with his guidance and respecting his quality control standards. He hired and trained Gerald Klug and the facility's doctor. The opening of this office later turned out to be a big problem. Shortly after its opening Dr. Klug notified him that the office was not adhering to Global's strict screening guidelines. Dr. DiLeo ordered it closed just six days after it opened. He instructed the office manager, Mark Artigues, to cease operations, close the doors, and dismantle the furniture and equipment.

By 2006 Dr. DiLeo decided that trying to live between New Orleans and Bradenton was not the lifestyle he imagined for himself. His work was in New Orleans, but his heart was in Florida. In January 2007 he resigned from Global and severed all relations with it. He had already accepted a position at the University of South Florida in the obstetrics and gynecology department with the title of Director, Division of Pelvic Pain. After resigning from Global, Dr. DiLeo was able to fill the position full time and was given free rein to develop novel protocols in this dynamic new field. Many of Dr. DiLeo's patients had been to several, as many as eight or ten doctors, before finding him. Some were sexual cripples; many thought they might be losing their mind. The doctor was able to cure many of these patients, and help restore healthy and productive lives, free of pain and able to establish healthy sex lives. The University had the status of being a leading facility throughout the world in research and innovation, and Dr. DiLeo was doing work that he loved.

Trouble began for Dr. DiLeo when complaints were lodged with LSBME against him and Dr. Pastorek by the mothers of two Global adult pain patients. In Dr. Pastorek's case the mother wanted him to stop treating her son because she claimed that the Lord would heal him, and his pain would go away. In the complaint against Dr. DiLeo, his patient strictly forbade him from speaking with his mother. The patient said his mother was completely crazy, and was posturing for a share of the money he had received from an accident that led to his painful condition. The doctors were prohibited by HIPPA laws (Health Information Patient Privacy Act) from discussing a patient's medical condition with anyone without permission of the patient. Both patients withheld permission.

The LSBME filed an administrative complaint against Dr. DiLeo in January 2007 even though he was living exclusively and practicing in Florida. Pursuant to the rules of LSBME, when an administrative complaint is lodged, the physician is given an opportunity to meet face-to-face with Dr. Mouton and the attorney for the Board, George Papale, in a process called a Bertucci hearing. The Bertucci invitation sounded like an opportunity to sit with Dr. Mouton and have a chat about the results of the investigation. But Dr. DiLeo's attorney, Herb Larson, told him, "Don't be fooled. These people are deadly serious and despite the tone of the letter, there is almost always a price to pay. The Board is focused on punishing doctors." In spite of the fact that Dr. DiLeo had already moved to Florida and had ceased practicing in Louisiana, he flew back to Louisiana to address Dr. Mouton and her attorney. In that meeting Dr. Mouton was icy cold to Dr. DiLeo and Herb Larson. She began by warning him, "To start off with, I want you to know that you have no credibility with me." That set the tone for what was to be an acrimonious meeting. George Papale yelled at Dr. DiLeo and Herb Larson. He was so out of control that it was actually Dr. Mouton, herself, who had to settle him down. Dr. DiLeo demonstrated that the medicine he was practicing was state of the art. He explained that the DEA had approved his methodology with respect to pain management and praised his success in being able to wean Global's patients off the highly addictive Xanax and Soma in favor of equally effective but less addictive alternatives. Dr. Mouton, instead of recognizing this conservative approach to pain management and the dispensing of strong medications, commented, "But it's not the DEA who is investigating you, is it." The meeting turned out to be a complete failure and the parties were unable to agree on anything. As is customary for Bertucci meetings, Dr. Mouton issued a consent decree against Dr. DiLeo, which set forth the State's allegations and Dr. DiLeo's punishment. Without admitting guilt, the doctor agreed to a fine of $5,000, and given a five-year probation to practice medicine in Louisiana, with restrictions on his license should he ever return to the state. The decree had no real effect on Dr. DiLeo, except for the fine, because he was no longer practicing in the state, and had no plans to ever do so again. In the matter of Dr. Pastorek and the mother who wanted the Lord to take over her son's case, the Board determined that no further actions were to be taken at that time. Timothy Lunch summed up Dr. Mouton's abuse of authority in a quote from his treatise "*First Principals of American Criminal Justice*" when he said, "The greatest dangers of liberty lurk in the insidious encroachment of men of zeal – well-meaning but without understanding."

In the medical profession a consent decree is a serious matter. When a decree is agreed upon it becomes public, Frequently suppliers, patients, creditors, admitting hospitals, and insurance carriers look for answers as to how this set of circumstances came about. In Dr. DiLeo's case, because of reciprocity laws, the State of Florida launched its own investigation. The Florida Board is particularly sensitive to accusations relating to the prescribing of pain medication, as that state has a reputation as the pill mill capitol, a reputation it goes to great lengths to shed. When the Florida investigation was complete, the Board determined that there was no impropriety, but it still assessed a fine of $5,000 and a one-year probation on his license. The only reason for the assessment was because he had been sanctioned in Louisiana.

During and after the unpleasant investigations and settlements with Louisiana and Florida, Dr. DiLeo continued his research and medical practice at the University. His reputation as an innovator in the treatment of pelvic pain was firmly established, and his portfolio of cured cases grew, as did his portfolio of babies delivered.

Another problem of greater proportions was brewing related to Global's Pensacola office. In spite of the fact that Dr. DiLeo had ordered that facility closed within days of its opening, unbeknownst to him, that office continued to operate for the next eighteen months. It had become a classic pill mill under Mark Artigues, with Dr. Klug as the supervising physician. The way Dr. DiLeo found out about it was from one of his patients who said he had been in the office in Pensacola recently. Dr. DiLeo told the patient that would be impossible, as the office had already closed. The patient corrected the doctor and told him that he had most certainly been treated in that office no more than two weeks earlier. By this time Dr. DiLeo was long gone from Global and Louisiana. Apparently, the order to close that office had been ignored.

After eighteen months of surveillance by the DEA, the bogus Global clinic in Pensacola (renamed Comprehensive Pain Care) was raided, and the agents confiscated all its records and computers. Meanwhile patients of that facility were carrying on a brisk drug trade, and several had died. It was assistant U.S. Attorney (AUSA) Randy Hansel of the Northern District of Florida who prosecuted the case. The investigation and prosecution led to guilty verdicts for Mark Artigues and Gerald Klug. Artigues pled guilty to conspiracy to prescribe drugs for other than medical purposed and money laundering, and was given an eighteen-year sentence. Dr. Klug fought the charges in court. He was found guilty as well and sentenced to three years in prison.

In 2008, in a grand jury media display, the Florida DEA, under orders from AUSA Hensel, raided the Louisiana Global offices. With cameras rolling and reporters taking it all in, the DEA agents carried out all the computers and medical records of more than 3,000 patients. All of the doctors in the office were pressured into surrendering their DEA prescription licenses on the spot. By 2009 AUSA Hensel had gone to the grand jury seeking indictments against Dennis Caroni and Doctors DiLeo and Pastorek, even though the two doctors had resigned from Global more than two years before the raid.

In an effort to obtain these indictments Mr. Hensel called a number of witnesses to give testimony before the grand jury, most of whom were extremely prejudiced in their testimony. Most of the witnesses were prior patients who had been dismissed from clinics as drug abusers. All had prior legal problems and something to gain by bearing false witness. One witness was a disgruntled former employee with an ax to grind. The most important witness, a prosecution witness, the one with the most intimate knowledge of the operation, was Marlena Angeletti, an employee of Global for years. Ms. Angeletti was asked to meet Mr. Hensel outside the grand jury room where he questioned her about the operations of Global. When she told him that Global was a fine organization worthy of praise, and tried to detail its fine qualities, Mr. Hensel said he couldn't use her and dismissed her. The grand jury never got to hear that side of the Global story.

Another witness, whose testimony was particularly damning, was John Johnson, the chief DEA investigator. In his statement to the grand jury he said he had examined all of the patient charts from the Global offices and that they were replete with evidence pointing to Dr. DiLeo and Dr. Pastorek's guilt. His testimony was particularly damning when he told the grand jury that he had seen evidence that Global was selling prescriptions, and performing shoddy physical exams or none at all. At trial Agent Johnson admitted that he did not examine those charts, but only a small percentage of them. The grand jury, therefore, acted upon false and misleading evidence.

When Herb Larson had left New Orleans for a temporary teaching job in Europe, Dr. DiLeo hired attorney Guy Womack to represent him. Mr. Womack was an experienced criminal defense lawyer who came very highly recommended. In June of 2010 Dr. DiLeo had heard nothing of the investigation for over a year and he believed that might be the end of it. He had been observing the legal issues relating to Global but never thought it was affecting him personally. But when Marlena Angeletti called to tell him of her brush with the grand jury, Dr. DiLeo called Womack to collect his thoughts on the situation. He was stunned to hear that his attorney believed him to be in jeopardy. "You're not out of it," said Womack, "your name is all over those charts." Dr. DiLeo asked him to call the prosecutor to find out if he was considered a witness or target. In the ensuing call Mr. Hensel told Womack, "There's a big red X on his back." There was no question about what that meant.

Investigator Johnson and Prosecutor Hensel intended to tie Dennis Caroni to the Comprehensive clinic in Pensacola. They then crossed two states to investigate and charge Global. Drs. DiLeo and Pastorek's names were tied to Global as practitioners, so they were also named in the indictment. Curiously, none of the doctors working at the Louisiana clinics at the time of the raid were indicted, leaving open the question of Johnson and Hensel's motivation. Further, the question of their authority and the case's venue remained unsettled.

Upon hearing this disturbing news about the investigation, it was determined that Attorney Womack should request a proffer meeting with Prosecutor Hensel. Dr. DiLeo had done nothing wrong and wanted to tell his story to the prosecutor. Hensel's reply was, "You'd better hurry," meaning, of course, that indictments would be coming soon. In the meeting with the prosecutor Dr. DiLeo laid out the entire working operation of Global and his involvement. He discussed the Pensacola office of which he was no part. Mr. Womack later commented that his testimony was concise, precise and convincing. Prosecutor Hensel's comment in summation was, "I don't buy it. I've heard it all before." He was alluding to the fact that Dr. Pastorek, in his meeting with LSBME, had told the same story. He was also admitting, without saying so, that he was not interested in the truth; he was only interested in convictions, and making a name for himself.

In July of 2010, based upon a great amount of false and misleading testimony, the grand jury returned a sealed indictment against Drs. Di Leo and Pastorek, and Dennis Caroni. But, since the indictments were sealed, none of those targeted, nor their attorneys were aware; and nothing came of it until October of that year. The action began at Chicago's O'Hare Airport as Dennis Caroni was waiting to board a plane to Israel. Agents of the U.S. Marshall's office pulled him out of line, arrested him, slapped handcuffs on him and escorted him from the premises in front of thousands of other travelers. Mr. Caroni was placed in a cell and denied bail throughout the entire process, arrest, trial, and sentencing. He was extradited to Florida, and from that day forward remained behind bars.

Dr. DiLeo heard from Guy Womack what had happened and was told to get ready. It wouldn't be long before they came for him. And he was right. The following morning three black Suburban SUVs showed up in the doctor's driveway and raided his home as if it were a fortified castle. Marshalls placed him under arrest and took him to the Federal Courthouse in Tampa. He spent several hours there before appearing before a federal magistrate and being released on a personal surety bond. By this time Dr. Pastorek had heard of the arrests and voluntarily surrendered to authorities. He was soon released on bond.

In order to be completely forthright and transparent with his employer, Dr. DiLeo went to his supervisors at USF to explain that he had been indicted and arrested. He did not want them to be surprised, or at a loss for a reaction when the news broke that one of their doctors had been arrested. He was fired on the spot and told to leave the facility immediately. When he explained that he had patients to see, he was told that someone would take care of that and to leave right away. After all the good work he had done there, the administration abandoned him completely. As the expression goes, they 'threw him under the bus'. Not only did the University dismiss Dr. Di Leo, but they also threatened that any untenured staff member who voluntarily testified for him, or acted as character witnesses on his behalf, would also be disciplined even to the extent that their jobs could be in jeopardy. Often in the medical field doctors' social contacts revolve around the hospital community. Being cut off from his friends, his colleagues and his income was devastating.

The following month Dr. DiLeo traveled to Pensacola, Florida, and entered a plea of not guilty in federal court. While Prosecutor Hensel argued that he would like to see the doctor never practice medicine again, the judge was more reasonable and worked with Guy Womack to structure an arrangement whereby Dr. DiLeo could continue to practice under supervision. The terms of that supervision were such that he was still able to perform surgeries, diagnosis, and therapeutics as before.

Two months after his dismissal from the University, Dr. DiLeo opened a private practice in beautiful Sarasota, not far from his home in Bradenton. Throughout most of 2011 he practiced in the area of gynecology and pelvic pain. Many of his patients came to him because he had treated them effectively while practicing at the University. Many others were secretly referred by physicians in the USF network because they believed in Dr. DiLeo's ability to treat pelvic pain, and there was nowhere better for patients with this affliction to go for state of the art medical treatment.

Twelve months following the indictments the trial began in the Federal Court House in Pensacola with Judge M. Casey Rodgers, the Chief Magistrate for the First Northwest Florida District, presiding. In a setback to the prosecution the judge ruled that information related to Comprehensive Pain Care (the former Pensacola office of Global) could not be used. And because the three defendants' cases had not been severed, all evidence and testimony from the LSBME was disallowed owing to the fact that Dennis Caroni was not a doctor, and was not subject to its jurisdiction. When Dr. Mouton was called as a prosecution witness, her testimony went no further than to say she was a doctor and the chief investigator for LSBME, a regulatory agency from another state. But these setbacks did not keep the prosecutor from putting on a six-week circus show before the judge and jury, a show that was fraught with lies, prejudicial remarks and planted evidence.

In preparation for the trial, Guy Womack called Jack Strain, the sheriff who hosted the summit meeting in St. Tammany Parish that brought in pain experts so the Parish could establish standards and protocols for dispensing pain medication. It was Sheriff Strain who had extended the invitation that resulted in the attendance of the two agents from the national headquarters of the DEA. But when Mr. Womack contacted him to request that he appear as a witness for Dr. DiLeo, the sheriff said he had no recollection of any such meeting. As an elected official sensitive to public opinion, it may have been seen as unpopular to be testifying on behalf of a "pill doctor". He certainly had changed his tune from the enthusiastic support he had given to Dr. DiLeo's idea three years earlier.

One obvious piece of evidence that could not have been legitimate was a letter in a medical patient's chart from the mother of one of Dr. DiLeo's patients beseeching him not to treat her son because he was a drug addict, and the treatment was only advancing his affliction. In a side conversation with his attorney (Dr. DiLeo did not take the witness stand personally) Dr. DiLeo contended that he had never seen that letter. Upon further examination it was determined that the letter had the wrong address on it so it could not be an authentic exhibit of the patient's chart. It must have been planted.

There were a number of prosecution witnesses who had no credibility at all. The first of these was Dr. Theodore Parran of Case Western University. His failure to maintain credibility as an expert witness began with him being an addictionologist, and not an expert in pain management. In fact, he had no credentials to qualify him to testify about that specialty. Out of more than 3,000 patient charts for the Global offices, he reviewed sixty-seven actual charts, all of which were selected because the patients had been rejected from the clinics and could present prejudicial testimony. He erred several times in his criticism of Dr. DiLeo's approach to examining patients. In one of these examples he said that the heart exams could only be performed when the patient was undressed wearing only a hospital gown, and in the supine position. In fact, nearly all heart exams of the kind needed for pain assessment are done with the patient clothed and in the sitting position. Dr. Parran further criticized the clinics for not performing Babinski reflex tests. He was way off base with that analysis. Babinski exams are performed on babies six months old or less. The exam takes place on the bottom of the infant's foot, which causes a reaction where the toes spread out and the big toe points up. That reaction does not appear in adults, and the test is not an indicator of anything in older patients except in the event of a stroke or head trauma. Nevertheless, the prosecutor pranced around the courtroom for weeks talking about failure to perform the Babinski exam. To a medical professional it was a foolish looking display, but the uninformed jury had no way of understanding that. In another blunder by Dr. Parran, he testified that Dr. DiLeo had inappropriately prescribed methadone to a patient who complained of pain in his mouth. Certainly, methadone would be the wrong solution to oral pain in any instance. But Dr. Parran misread the doctor's recommendation. Instead of methadone, Dr. DiLeo had recommended mouthwash. Dr. Parran sat on the witness stand for six days giving testimony against Drs. DiLeo and Pastorek, most of the time not being in tune at all with reality.

When an expert witness for the defense appeared, she shredded Dr. Parran's testimony. Dr. Carol Warfield was Chairperson of the Department of Pain Management at Harvard University School of Medicine. She testified that Dr. DiLeo's procedures were exemplary. When asked about Dr. Parran's testimony she replied, "I don't know where he gets this stuff."

The second witness of questionable credibility, and one that caused considerable damage to the defense with his lies, was DEA Agent Johnson. In the grand jury hearing he testified that he had reviewed all of the 3,000 plus charts of Global's patients, and found them replete with errors and lacking medical information necessary to make accurate determination of the patients' needs. He steered his testimony in such a way as to give the impression that Global was operating exclusively for the purpose of writing and selling prescriptions for unnecessary opioids for profit. The grand jury had bought his testimony and it was in large part on account of this that it indicted the defendants. Under questioning it was discovered that instead of examining 3,000 charts, he had actually only reviewed about thirty. When confronted with the question as to whether he lied to the grand jury or was he lying to the court, he said he was telling the court the truth. Perhaps had he told the truth to the grand jury there never would have been an indictment.

The trial lasted six weeks. Attorney Hensel had to dumb down in his summation in order to appear to the jury that he was speaking the same language its members spoke. The jurors were a cross section of blue-collar types from the deep south (north Florida). With statements from the prosecution like, "We don't need no Harvard professors with their fancy books to come down here and tell us what's right and what's wrong," referring to the testimony of Dr. Carol Warfield, the appeal to their cultural and educational limitations could not be denied. The jury was exhausted, and everybody just wanted to go home.

Then came the day that Judge Rodgers gave instructions to the jury. It was the Wednesday before Thanksgiving 2011. She told the jury that she expected it to take five days just to review the evidence. But it was the day before a four-day holiday and the members of the jury were ready to go home, to be done with this trial, and to return to their normal lives. It took only two hours for the jury to elect a foreman, eat dinner, review over twenty-five pages of jury instructions, and come back with a hastily crafted verdict. All three men, Dennis Caroni, Dr. DiLeo, and Dr. Pastorek were found guilty of conspiracy to prescribe drugs for other than legitimate reasons. Dr. DiLeo and Dennis Caroni were also found guilty of money laundering. The sentencing was set for eight months later, July 2012. Dennis Caroni returned to jail, and Drs. DiLeo and Pastorek were released on their previously established bonds.

When the time for sentencing arrived, Judge Rodgers chose to further delay her rulings. She explained that she had too much evidence to ponder. She wanted to be clear on her facts and she particularly wanted to fully understand the impacts of Dr. Parran's mistakes and mistruths, and the effect they may have had on the jury's verdict. The sentencing was eventually reset for January 2013, six months later.

During this six-month recess Dr. DiLeo used the time to continue his normal family functions. He also created a forty-five-minute video entitled "A Day in the Life." The video featured Luke's special condition and the family's need to constantly watch over him. Suffering from cerebral palsy and blindness, confined to a wheel chair, he could never be left alone. A harsh sentence for Dr. DiLeo would mean inestimable hardships for his family as well.

It is quite possible that at sentencing Judge Rodgers was swayed by this video and by Dr. Pastorek's impassioned speech about his own son's special needs. Further, family and friends were in attendance to lend support. Dr. Anna Parsons, a tenured professor at University of South Florida, who worked alongside Dr. DiLeo, and was familiar with his successes in healing suffering patients, spoke in support of him. His brother, John, an anesthesiologist, spoke at the professional level as well.

But the judge remained unimpressed with Dennis Caroni. He was not a good person to have as a co-defendant. He was unpolished and sloppy looking, and made a bad impression with his bruskness and poor manners. It would have been difficult for a jury to like him. Those qualities may have ended up costing him in the end. He was sentenced to twenty years in prison. Dr. Pastorek received a sentence of one year and one day.

At the age of sixty-one, Dr. DiLeo received a sentence of twenty-four months in federal prison followed by three years of supervised release. But time in prison doesn't really tell the whole story. This episode not only cost him time in jail, but it cost him his job and his license to practice medicine. It forced him into bankruptcy and into having the family home foreclosed upon. It cost him separation from his family that was left suffering and needing him badly. His scheduled release was September 2014, but he didn't know what he could do to earn a living and provide for his family when he became a free man again.

All this heartache and pain, all on account of an ambitious prosecutor and clueless jury. All this destruction to a career and a family and all those years of study, hard work, dedication and hope, to be dashed, proving how unevenly yoked the punishment is in relation to the crime, or no crime at all. And injustice like this will continue to happen to good people like Dr. DiLeo until something is done to curb the voracious appetites of the U.S. Department of Justice.

Alex Kozinski, a judge for the U.S. Court of Appeals for the 9th Circuit, summed it up when he declared, "The malevolent prosecutor, empowered by ubiquitous criminal penalties and harsh sentences, will have broad authority to punish almost anyone he chooses. This power will be especially dangerous if seized upon by an aspiring tyrant."

David and the Goliath
The Story of David Wenchyu Liou

The story goes, "What should you do if you enroll in a college course that is graded on the curve, and you find there is a Chinese student in the class?" The answer, "Drop the class." This amusing anecdote is a reference to how well Chinese students perform in the American college system. The competition among these students for placement in U.S. universities is fierce, and only a fractional percentage of those who apply are accepted. David Wenchyu Liou is one of those exceptional people.

David was born in 1936 in China's Jiangsu Province. His early life was marked by adversity of the Sino-Japanese War wherein the Japanese army conquered and occupied two thirds of the China mainland. David's father, Liu Chishun, was a graduate of the Chinese military academy at Huang Pu, the equivalent of America's West Point. The headmaster at the time was Chaing Kai Shek who later became the leader of the Chinese Nationalist Party. Among Chin Shun's instructors was Chou En Lai who later became the Chinese premier concurrent with the Communist Party Chairmanship of Mao Tse Tung. David grew up during the time of the Sino-Japanese War, a time when his father commanded battalions, as many as 100,000 troops, as the Japanese army advanced through the country in a bloody imperialistic campaign. On July 7, 1937, just about a half year after David's birth, China declared war on Japan hoping to resist that treacherous aggression.

David remembers those years when his family had to continually migrate south through the country to stay ahead of the Japanese assault. In the middle of the night soldiers of the Nationalist Army would come to assist the family in packing up and moving to the next location. By the time the Japanese surrendered in 1945 David had attended twenty or more primary schools, some for as little as a couple of weeks. A few taught in dialects other than David's native Mandarin. Often David would sit in class not understanding a word that was spoken. But in spite of these interruptions he was an exceptional student, although he regrets that his lessons in English had been interrupted for several years leaving him at a disadvantage when he later moved to the U.S. to study.

During the Chinese civil war, pitting Mao's Communist forces against Chaing Kai Shek's Nationalist Army, Chin Shun served as a lieutenant general on the Nationalist side. In this bitter struggle millions of soldiers and civilians were killed. By the time the communist forces crossed the Yangtze River, it was known that the struggle to keep China from falling into the hands of the communists was lost. Chin Shun moved his family away from China to the island of Formosa, which today is known as Taiwan.

Although the worrying for his father's welfare never ceased, a certain orderliness entered David's life and he was able to concentrate on his studies with renewed energy. As an exceptional student, David was selected to attend university in Taiwan where he studied chemical engineering and participated in the military equivalent of ROTC. Upon graduation, with highest honors, he was commissioned as a lieutenant in the army. Upon completion of his two-year military obligation, David flew to America to do studies in chemical engineering. He took post-graduate courses at the University of Virginia, and did a summer internship with Dow Chemical. In 1964 he received a Master of Science Degree in chemical engineering from the Illinois Institute of Technology.

David was working for Fairbanks Morse after graduation when he was contacted by people he had worked with at Dow. The company remembered him from his internship and wanted him to become a part of their future. He accepted the position at Dow and went to work doing polymer research at its headquarters in Midland, Michigan. After eight years in research, Dow sent David to MIT, where he studied computer applications of chemical engineering processes. Here David studied under the famous professor Dr. John Evans. Eleven years into his career at Dow he was sent to the Netherlands, where for five years he held the title of Manager of Polymer Research. In this capacity he had about twenty engineers and chemists under him as they worked on the development of engineering plastics. From the Netherlands David was transferred to Dow's Plaquemine, Louisiana, research facility where he was a Scientist working on new inventions. Dow had 10,000 researchers worldwide, of which only about 1% held the title 'Scientist'. Almost never does Dow promote a researcher to Scientist unless he holds a PhD degree. They recruit heavily from the best universities. But David was that rare exception, the fractional part of 1% of all researchers who could rise to the title of Scientist without a doctoral degree. Six of Dow's patents were David's inventions including his contribution to the invention of the Ziploc bag. In 1992, after 28 years of service, David retired from Dow at the age of 55.

After a year of disappointing idleness in retirement, David decided to pursue a career in private practice as a chemical engineering consultant. He opened his own consulting company. With his exceptional knowledge in the area of polymer research, and strong business and family connections in his homeland China, David had found a place where he could turn his life's work into a profitable venture. A fellow Dow retiree by the name of John Wheeler joined David in this venture. In Beijing, China, they set up a research facility in cooperation with several Chinese university professors. This lab was designed to produce a rubber-like substance called chlorosulfinated polyethylene

(CSPE) for which David received a patent in 1997. CSPE was a product in high demand. It could be used in the manufacture of high-pressure hoses, and as a jacket for banded electrical cables. It was flexible and durable, and resistant to cold, heat and ultraviolet rays, and just as important; its manufacturing process was non-polluting. David could envision this product being used under the hood and throughout the interiors of millions of automobiles. This was a time when China's demand for materials of this nature was booming.

In a civil complaint filed by Dow Chemical in 1999 it claimed that David's firm had employed its patented trade secrets in the process of developing CSPE. It claimed that the feedstock of CSPE used in its development was protected by patents and trade secrets. That feedstock was chlorinated polyethylene (CPE). CPE is a generic product of which there are various methods of production and different formulas for the combining of chlorine and polyethylene. Much like baking a cake or building a car, there are chocolate cakes, velvet cakes and banana cakes. There are Fords, Chevys and Mitsubishis. There are hundreds of different types of CPE. Nothing on the open market was suitable for David's CSPE product; he had to invent his own. He created a unique process for CPE and had it patented. It was nothing like anything Dow or anybody else produced. What Dow never disclosed was that it had obtained its license for CPE in the 1960s from Hoechst Company of Germany. Dow did develop a CPE-like product just outside Hoechst's patented claims and proceeded to have it patented. In the 1980s Hoechst decided to cease CPE production and sold its process technology and plant facilities to a chemical company in China. Dow's patent for its CPE-like product expired in 1988. By this time more than 100 companies in China were producing CPE as all of the patents had expired, and its product and process were now in the public domain. Since CPE was no longer protected by patents, it could no longer be classified as a trade secret. In the civil case and under oath, John Wheeler testified that the lab and process design were in no way modeled after Dow's plant or processes.

In heated discussions between David's attorneys and Dow's attorneys, Dow made outrageous, draconian demands. In order to put an end to the complaint Dow demanded that David never have contact with Dow employees, either current or previous employees. This demand infuriated David. Many of his friends were people he had worked with at Dow. And what was he to do about Katherine, his wife? She was also a previous employee of Dow. Further, David was to cease engaging in chemical engineering, the profession that he had studied and worked at all his life. He would further be required to notify Dow of any planned travel abroad, and he would have to report to Dow on his daily activities every six months. In a deposition related to the case, attorneys for Dow said that if David did not agree to its terms they would "litigate him into the grave." But David was an innocent man and he was not going to be swayed by these bullying tactics. He summarily rejected their demands. The battle between Dow and David went on for six years. Dow had asked for a speedy trial to begin with, but the legal arguments continued. With the daunting prospects of a never-ending legal battle, where the costs had gone out of control, Dow fired the Business Director who initiated the lawsuit. It would use its influence with the Justice Department to have the Grand Jury go after David in a criminal case. This dirty play by Dow, which had access to an already broken justice system, worked to David's extreme disadvantage. Dow stopped pursuing its civil action against him. No trial date was ever set and no judgment was ever entered.

When asked why Dow initiated this suit when there was no intention of pursuing it, David says, "I believe there are two reasons for this. First, they wanted to use me as an example so that high-ranking technical people in the company don't retire and try to take company secrets with them. I believe this very public and humiliating experience has served its purpose. But even more sinister, Dow's efforts to compete in the worldwide market for CPE had turned into a dismal failure. It cost Dow about $1,400 per ton to produce it, plus the cost of transporting it. The Chinese import duties drove the cost to the consumer up to about $1,800 per ton. Competitors in China were delivering the same product at $1,100 per ton making it impossible for Dow to make a profit or to break even. They took a two-pronged approach. First they began dumping CPE on the Chinese market at $800 per ton in violation of trade treaties and international law. But this losing position could not go on for long as it was affecting their bottom line. A decision was made to close their CPE production plant in Plaquemine. It would mean shutting down one of their divisions at a cost they calculated to be $268 million. Instead of owning up to the fact that their process was inefficient, non-competitive and polluting, they chose to blame the Chinese for putting them out of business. It was a public relations ploy. After all, hundreds of workers and researchers were going to be reassigned, transferred, or phased out. It had to appear a certain way in the press. They pursued the story about the Chinese competition and placed me at the middle of it. The truth was that the only CPE I produced was a different formula from any produced by Dow, and I never sold it. I only used it for feedstock in the production of my own product, CSPE."

Although Dow did not aggressively pursue their $268 million claim against David, they had set him up as an example to others. They destroyed what should have been a peaceful retirement of a loyal employee, and they devastated him financially. They sent seven trial lawyers after him, and he responded with a team of his own. But Dow is the 800-pound gorilla with billions of dollars in resources to pursue individuals, and do so with impunity. Dow spent six years and five million dollars pursuing this case. David is just one man, and at times his legal fees were as much as $170,000 per month. His resources were soon depleted, and the peace in his life, and that of his family and friends, was shattered.

In 2006, while living in Shanghai, at the age of 72, David became critically ill. He began retaining fluids and his heart rate rose dramatically. Several doctors had mis-diagnosed his condition and began treating him with the wrong medications. By the time they had discovered that pericarditis had set in he was in critical condition. Of his condition David says, "The lower half of my body looked like that of a Sumo wrestler. My upper half degenerated to where I looked like a Holocaust survivor. My resting heart rate was 120 beats per minute." Pericarditis is an inflammation of the pericardium, the sac that surrounds the heart. It often results in death if not immediately and properly treated. Believing that he could be better treated by specialists at the Heart Center of Houston Hospital, an emergency evacuation was arranged.

On a stopover in Seattle, David, able to move only by means of a wheelchair, was greeted by three FBI agents who took him into custody. He had no previous knowledge that a grand jury indictment had been issued. Assistant U.S. Attorney (AUSA) for the middle district of Louisiana, Ian Hipwell, had secured the indictment in which fourteen criminal counts were cited. David was facing 330 years in prison and fines in the amount of $8.7 million. He was not granted bail and was taken into custody immediately. David and Katherine were floored. David's condition worsened and Katherine was left to worry about what this night and the following days might bring, or even if David was strong enough to live through the night. He was taken to two different jails that would not admit him because they did not have facilities that could accommodate a person in his condition. He was taken to a hospital, but it too rejected him. He ultimately spent the night in jail.

Meanwhile Katherine phoned David's daughter, Caroline, who was living in Beijing. Caroline had contacts in the U.S. and through friends was able to arrange for an emergency appearance before a magistrate the following morning. The result was that David was released and allowed to continue on to the hospital in Houston. His open-heart surgery was successful and after a month in the hospital, and six month's recovery at his sister's home in Houston, he was allowed to return to his Louisiana home. Here he faced charges of conspiracy to steal trade secrets.

The noise that Dow had made with the civil suit had caught the attention of the federal authorities and they chose to pursue criminal charges. For four years David's attorneys attempted to discover what information the feds had to support these charges. Not until ten days before the trial did the prosecutor release the information so David and his attorneys would know what they were facing. David is and always has been a peaceful and quiet man. These charges devastated him and his family.

Testifying against David was John Wheeler, the very man who stated under oath on ten previous occasions that none of Dow's processes were used in the manufacture of CSPE. Now he had reversed his story and stated that he had in fact copied some of Dow's work flow information. His story was that he had retained in memory information and documentation related to the production of CPE that Dow had previously published. That published information was already in the public domain. But his statement that he used Dow's processes from that publication was interpreted by the prosecution as an admission of the use of Dow's trade secrets. Even though David was producing his own CPE, and using it only as feedstock for CSPE, the prosecution stretched the truth to the breaking point to make it look like the CSPE product could not have been formulated without Dow's proprietary formulas. In fact, at this time, hundreds of companies throughout the world were producing CPE using many dozens of different formulae, and ending up with many different kinds of CPE. "The government must have scared Wheeler into changing his story," says David. "I believe he was told there would be a reward for his cooperation; that reward being a one year probation in lieu of the punishment I was facing. It is hard to believe the government prosecutors can have so much power to have witnesses lie under oath in order to avoid punishment such as I received."

Convinced of his innocence, David would not entertain an offer of a plea bargain. In defense of his honor and reputation as a celebrated scientist, he would fight to clear his good name. So, at the age of 75, depressed and in marginal health, David launched his defense against fourteen criminal counts. He put forth a logical and convincing argument that none of the charges had merit. On the opposite side, the prosecutor sought a maximum penalty of five years in prison and restitution to be paid to Dow. But in a three-week trial, and in spite of his being on the right side of the argument, the jury returned a guilty verdict of a single count of conspiracy. He was sentenced to five years in prison, three years of probation, and restitution to be determined.

In restitution hearings subsequent to the trial Dow demanded $268 million, a figure calculated as the revenue they lost by the closing of their CPE plant in Plaquemine. It remains a mystery as to what Dow was thinking with such an outrageous demand. David was a simple man living in retirement with limited resources. Dow and the prosecutors had already depleted his life savings and assets through the legal proceedings. And now a seventy-five year old man was going to prison. Such a demand was an outrageous abuse of the court system. And in restitution hearings the judge agreed. Dow withdrew its demand, and the attorneys and court agreed on a $600,000 forfeiture of assets. It cost David his two homes, his retirement account and his life savings.

At 77 years of age, David Wenchyu Liou, broke and broken after seven decades of honorable hard work and service, entered the Federal Prison Camp at Pensacola, Florida, to begin serving a five-year sentence. His family continued to support him; his wife and daughter visited for a few hours each week, and David remained hopeful that at eighty years of age, when freed from prison, that he would be able to return to the outside where he could spend his remaining years free to enjoy the warm embrace of his wife and children. Unfortunately Dow Chemical and the federal prosecutors will have gained nothing, and their vulgar behavior will be allowed to go on as if nothing happened.

Political Corruption and Prosecutorial Abuse
In an Alabama Court Case
United States of America vs. John W. Goff

To begin his journey to the Federal Prison Camp at Pensacola, Florida, sixty-five year old Alabama insurance executive John Goff underwent "Diesel Therapy." Diesel Therapy is a term used around the Bureau of Prisons (BOP) to describe their way of breaking down an inmate's spirit by moving him   between institutions on his way to his final destination. In John's case he self-surrendered to the prison in Montgomery and was transported by van to the Lee County, Alabama, lockup where he spent his first two weeks of incarceration. Next, with handcuffs and ankle shackles, he boarded another prison bus for transport to the notorious Federal Detention Center in Atlanta, Georgia. FDC Atlanta has a reputation as one of the worst places an inmate can land anywhere in the federal BOP system. Ask about Atlanta and inmates can only shake their heads and say, "There's no place like it." In Atlanta John was placed in the general population where every kind of dangerous felon resides, and where lockdown was for twenty-three hours a day. Ten days later the shackles were applied again and John boarded the BOP's transport plane, commonly referred to as 'Con Air', for a ten day stay at BOP central, the medium security facility in Oklahoma City. From O.C. John was again transported courtesy of Con Air to the federal prison at Oakdale, Louisiana, where he stayed for about one year. At this facility John was informed that he was over his security limit, meaning he was being kept in a higher level of security than merited by his profile. He should have been in a prison camp instead of a low security level facility (called a 'low'). He was moved to a single cell for his own protection, the only inmate out of 1,200 in the prison to have this treatment. From Oakdale John was released with a temporary furlough to self-surrender at the Federal Prison Camp at Pensacola, Florida. The Diesel Therapy had its intended result of wearing John down and keeping him from having effective communication with the outside world. He arrived in Pensacola exhausted and dispirited.

Years later John remained in prison. His daily routine consisted of rising at 5:00 a.m. to stand in line for a breakfast of grits or bran flakes, and an apple if he's lucky. Each morning John visited the chapel library for an hour or two where he could read or watch inspirational videos to keep his spirits high and attitude positive. Later in the morning there was a lunch of over-cooked hot dogs or hamburgers. If it's Thursday he might get bread, a small salad, and a piece of chicken. In the early afternoon John would work at the camp laundry where he helped to sort and hand out prison uniforms. He also worked in the recycling department, and on kitchen detail. On account of his age, his workday lasted only three hours. For his work, this man who at one time was earning a million dollars a year, was now earning twelve cents an hour, less than a half dollar a day. After work John joined the chow line again and hoped for relief from a diet heavy in potatoes, rice, and beans.

But not everything at FPC Pensacola was awful. There was time to read, watch news and sports on TV, exercise, check emails, and attend limited classes and religious services. But going from being Johnny Dollar, the center of the universe in Alabama insurance circles, to taking orders from corrections officers who wouldn't even be allowed to carry his briefcase on the outside, was a humbling, humiliating step down. He went from custom-made suits to an ill-fitting utility uniform and heavy work boots.

The place John lived in had ten men in an old military barrack quad built for two enlisted servicemen. He stood for several prison counts each day, and was surrounded day and night by the sights and sounds of heavily tattooed gang brothers speaking Spanish and Ebonics, and making noise twenty four hours a day, seven days a week. Hours turned into days, days became years, and the years continued to slowly roll by. From the moment of his indictment by U.S. Attorney Leura Canary, John's life was in a downward spiral from the pinnacle of respectability and achievement in the world of commerce, to the depths of existence, incarcerated along side common criminals and the lowest echelon of uncultured society. The journey was long and tragic, and life would have never turned out this way if not for the actions of politically motivated individuals, a few friends who betrayed John's trust, and a criminal justice system that can be manipulated by a few powerful and corrupt politicians and their supporters (lobbyists and bagmen).

Born in 1948 in Montgomery, Alabama, John grew up in an upper middle class environment. His father owned several successful furniture businesses called Homa - Goff Furniture Company. It was a privileged life with a lovely home in Montgomery and a beach house in Florida. All the necessities of life were well provided for, including an excellent education culminating in a business education from Auburn University and the University of Alabama. As an idealistic child of the 1960s, as opposed to trying to change the world through marches and protest, John saw the greatest opportunity to make a positive difference through government service and politics. In his mid twenties he joined the staff of the very popular four-time Alabama Governor George Wallace. John believed in the work that the governor was doing and wanted to see him be the successful candidate for President of the United States.

In the 1972 Democratic campaign for president, George Wallace was a strong competitor. Not only was he the most popular candidate in the South, but he had also made strong inroads in the Midwest and West. John had by this time become a senior aide and trusted supporter of the governor. He worked as an advance man for the campaign directly under the campaign manager, Charles Snider. Everything was going well, actually better than well, for Wallace's campaign until that fateful day in Laurel, Maryland, when would-be assassin, Arthur Bremmer, pumped five bullets into the governor. Bremmer had been stalking Wallace for quite some time, and when the opportunity presented itself, he changed the course of history.

John heard the news of the assassination attempt when he landed in Portland, Oregon, to make ready for a Wallace campaign stop. He called Charles Snider to ask for instructions and was told to hold a press conference to tell the media that Wallace was alive and the campaign would proceed. A weakened Governor Wallace started to regain some of his health after the attack but never fully recovered. As a senior aide and close associate of the governor, John attended the 1972 Democratic Convention in Miami Beach. Governor George McGovern won that nomination and became the democratic candidate for President. Meanwhile John was promoted to executive assistant to the Governor, a very prestigious post in which he served for two more years. As the governor's political life trailed off, John lost interest in politics and decided to find another path for his life.

His brief career in state politics afforded John the opportunity to rub elbows with some very influential people, both in the political arena and in business. Among those prominent people was John Amos, the founder of AFLAC Insurance Company. Amos used to tell John that he had been teased by other insurance industry executives about payroll deduction policies where the monthly premium could be as low as $10 per month. Amos response to that was, "Maybe the premiums are only $10 per month, but I have

8,000,000 customers." His encouragement and fabulous stories about success in the insurance business piqued John's interest. He decided to open his own agency. Amos had always told John that he saw in him an honest and open manner, an agreeable sales personality, and the intelligence and contacts to be successful.

For much of John's career Amos had been a business associate and mentor. Although Amos had an established business that was earning well and growing rapidly, John had something Amos saw as key to a successful future in insurance. John, through his years of working in the governor's office, knew people. He had established contacts at every level of government from city fathers, to county commissioners, to House and Senate representatives in Montgomery. These contacts connected to school boards, other branches of public work, and anyone in the private sector who did business with these people. This was a gold mine of connections that Amos could turn into policy premiums.

In 1974 the Goff Agency, Inc. opened its doors for business in Montgomery. The office was a single room that John rented in the Union Bank Building on Commerce Street. It was furnished with a desk and chairs he brought in from home. It had an answering machine, but no assistants, and no secretary. It was just John on his own, wearing down the shoe leather to write business, and training himself to be the rainmaker for much bigger things to come. The company developed into a multi-line life and health agency. John Amos gave John access to the AFLAC payroll deduction plan. All John had to do was use his contacts with other agents to come into their organizations to present the AFLAC product. It was the marriage of John's Rolodex to AFLAC's product line. John's army of agents began to grow as it signed up hundreds of organizations, universities, counties, cities, school boards, and private companies. Soon large commissions began to flow into the Goff Group. Within five years hundreds of thousands of policies were in force, which became the launch pad for future growth of the Goff insurance empire.

In the 1980s Amos came to John with a prediction that a crash was coming in the workers' comp area. As it turned out, the prediction came true. In 1992 John formed the Professional Business Owners Association. As a result, heterogeneous workers' comp funds were formed in Alabama and North Carolina. Out of chaos came opportunity for the person who was prepared. Amos helped John prepare by showing him how to capitalize on the coming crisis. And Amos's advice was good. As individual workers' comp companies began limiting availability of that product, there was no alternative but to have states create assigned risk pools. In 1996 John founded the Pinnacle Casualty Assurance Company. It was one of the only domestic insurance carriers in Alabama licensed to offer workers' comp policies.

By the 1990s John had grown the Goff Group, with state of the art billing and claims technology, and the finest staff in the state for administering workers' comp insurance policies. The Group was licensed in fifty states and was thus able to insure every worker in Alabama, regardless of the location of their company's home state.

Mickey DeBellis was the Alabama State Insurance Commissioner during this time. DeBellis was an exceptionally fine insurance commissioner and his career spanned twenty years and the governorships of three administrations, a feat nearly unheard of in Alabama for an appointed cabinet position. He often called John when he needed a professional opinion related to insurance. DeBellis saw the wreckage that other states had created in allowing multiple agencies handle their workers' comp assigned risk pools and he wanted to avoid that result. The Goff Group qualified, and was named the sole administrator of the Alabama Workers' Comp Depop Assigned Risk Pool. By 1996 the assigned risk business, which was just a part of the Goff portfolio, was responsible for $400 million per year in premium billings.

By the turn of the millennium the Goff Group had six offices throughout the country and Bermuda. Its home office in Montgomery employed 200 insurance professionals, and the company had 18,000 agents nationwide. The Goff Group companies included: Goff Group, Inc.; Southern Brokerage Services, Inc.; Medical Claims Management, Inc.; Goff Capital Ltd. (Hamilton, Bermuda); Goff Group Investments, Inc. (Real Estate); Pinnacle Casualty Assurance Corporation, and Pinnacle Assurance Group. John also owner Goff Aviation, Inc. (for management of the company jet) but left it outside the umbrella of the Goff Group, Inc. for liability purposes.

John Goff, by this time nicknamed "Johnny Dollar" by friends and industry associates, was the biggest name in the insurance industry in the state of Alabama, and maybe the south. He had built one of the finest insurance organizations in the nation, had sealed his reputation as one of the leading and best-connected entrepreneurs in Alabama, and had amassed a personal fortune estimated in the neighborhood of $50 million.

Through all the years of growth and success, the Goff Group relied on the Montgomery branch of the Birmingham law firm of Haskell, Slaughter to handle its legal affairs. Tommy Gallion was the attorney for the firm assigned to the Goff account. Through the years Tom Gallion and John Goff became best of friends. Tom was proud to refer to John as his "little brother'. He wanted people to know that he was the confidant and best friend to the biggest insurance man in the state. John was just as happy with the arrangement, and he relied on Gallion's advice before making any moves that could have legal ramifications. John entertained Gallion at his home, his farm, and his beach house many times. They attended social events, sporting events, and public and private functions together scores of times. When John took a trip on the corporate jet, Tommy Gallion was often along. On the professional side, John estimates that over the years the billing from the Haskell, Slaughter, and Gallion firm amounted to many millions of dollars.

Just prior to the 2002 gubernatorial campaign Gallion suggested that John hire a part time lobbyist to handle the Goff Group's relationship with the state insurance department. Even though the Goff Group enjoyed an excellent relationship with the State, Gallion was able to convince John to hire Ferrell Patrick. Patrick was a lobbyist and strong supporter of republican gubernatorial candidate, Bob Riley. Gallion's argument was that the Goff Group's relationship with the state would be further cemented.

What John did not know at the time was just how underhanded Patrick and his political allies were capable of being. Along the way Patrick convinced John, who had little interest in politics, to support Riley in his campaign for governor. John held a fundraiser for Riley and invited wealthy and well-connected people from his circle of influence to attend. He even authorized Patrick to allow the governor's campaign to use the company jet for appearances within the state. Not long thereafter John hired Patrick as a full time employee, allowing him also to continue his lobbying work. It would not be long before John would learn that Patrick had abused his authority with respect to the company plane, and that his influence with state regulators had a negative effect. Patrick was also disliked by most of his co-workers within the Goff Group. Friends and business associates warned John to fire Patrick and sever any relationship he had with him. Ferrell Patrick was a pariah who was bringing John down.

In the 2002 campaign for the Alabama governor's office, Bob Riley was a somewhat uninspired candidate. In his favor was the fact that the Republican Party liked him and could envision him as just the kind of puppet governor it could control. As a used car salesman and former congressman with limited popularity, Riley needed a big boost to run his campaign. By this time the term of Steve Windom, the former Lieutenant Governor under the very popular Governor Don Siegelman, had expired. Windom had parlayed his influence into a lobbying career, and was a big supporter of Riley's in the campaign. But both Windom and Riley knew that campaigns are run on money, and money is gotten through favors. But where to parlay his future power into immediate dollars was the question. His answer came in the form of a contribution to the republican campaign fund from Washington lobbyist Jack Abramoff. Abramoff represented the Mississippi Choctaw Indian gaming interests.

In Alabama, businessman Milton McGregor owned the biggest bingo operation. There were others, but McGregor was the biggest. His Victoryland halls were not your Thursday night church parlor. It was a sophisticated gambling operation that was taking in millions of dollars, and attracting gamblers from Alabama and other nearby states. And Victoryland was a threat to the Mississippi Choctaw Indians' action just across the river. Riley promised that in return for $13 million in campaign contributions, he would seek legislation to halt the bingo operations in Alabama.

Earlier John had granted limited authorization for the Republican Party to use his jet for campaign purposes. His intended in-kind contribution was supposed to be limited to campaign stops within the state. Unbeknownst to John, the Goff jet that was used to fly to Washington on two different occasions without his authorization. John believes those trips were made, in part, to facilitate the relationship between Riley and. When John heard that his plane had been used twice to fly to Washington he recoiled. He informed the plane manager, Ferrell Patrick, that this was outside the bounds of his authority, and an inappropriate use of the plane. He sent a bill to the Riley campaign for $25,000. The Republican Governors Association paid the freight for Riley; a check in the amount of $17,000, and another for $8,000.

Bob Riley won the 2002 election for Governor. In January 2003 he took office and began to pay back the cronies, lobbyists and bagmen who helped to get him elected. There was a new sheriff in town and those people doing business with the state were going to have to pay to play. It is the governor's prerogative to appoint his own cabinet when he takes office, and Riley used that power in ways that previous governors could not have imagined. One of the prestigious cabinet positions was that of insurance commissioner. That job went to Walter Bell with the recommendation of Steve Windom.

Ferrell Patrick and another Goff employee, CFO Mike Marsh, approached Steve Windom with a scheme to shake down the Goff organization. Having no integrity or appreciation for the body of work that John had created, and the generous salaries he paid them, they devised a plan that would help them share in the Goff empire's hard earned wealth. Steve Windom liked their idea and decided to run with it. The plan involved Windom, Patrick, and March, and two of Windom's close associates, Jim Tait and Don Price. They conspired to create an arrangement whereby they could participate in profits of the Goff/Alabama assigned risk pools.

Jim Tait called John and asked for a meeting, and John consented. At the appointed time only Tait and Price arrived. In that meeting Tait told John that Steve Windom controlled the insurance department and the new commissioner, Walter Bell. John had no reason to doubt that. He was told that he could keep the Alabama assigned risk pool business if he would give 50% of the proceeds from that line to the new organization that was to be formed for the benefit of Tait, Price, Patrick, and Marsh. John listened to the extortion attempt, and did what any adroit businessman would do, he asked for time to think about it, and sent the men on their way.

Before Tait and Price had left the building John was on the phone to Tommy Gallion to tell him what had just happened. John's inclination was to ignore or refuse the extortion attempt even if it meant losing the assigned risk business. First of all, he felt confident that there was no one in the state who was equipped to take the Goff Group's place in the administration of that insurance line. And second, he refused to be extorted or involved in dirty politics. He had hoped to someday turn the business over to his son, and he did not want it to be tainted by an association with Bob Riley, Bill Canary, Walter Bell, or Steve Windom.

But in that attempted shakedown, Gallion saw an opportunity for another one of his clients, Milton McGregor. Of course the Goff business was significant for the Haskell, Slaughter law firm, and there was the personal relationship between Gallion and Goff. But Goff's billings paled in comparison to the McGregor account. Gallion had to chose his allegiance. Even in the face of ethical violations and legal malpractice, he chose to chase the money with the agreement of the firm's Birmingham home office. If Gallion could recover McGregor's lost gaming interests he would be a hero, and a very wealthy man. To do so he would have to take down the Riley administration. John knew none of this information at the time, and he continued to rely on Gallion's counsel all the way through his indictment and trial.

When John refused Windom's strong-arm tactics, the state insurance department turned up the heat. Under Commissioner Bell's authority the department filed a complaint charging the Goff Group with sixty violations. It posted these charges on its web site and sent press releases to the two most important industry magazines, Business

Insurance and National Underwriter. The bad news spread rapidly. Stories in newspapers and on the Internet carried tales of the Goff Group engaging in such activities as withholding premiums from carriers, defrauding churches and individuals, and even cheating the revered Auburn University, which the Goff Group never even insured.

Mike Bounds was counsel for the Department at the time. When he heard of the charges he told Commissioner Bell that John, by statute, was entitled to a hearing before the charges should be made public. Bell ignored his warning and posted the charges anyhow, and never granted John the hearing he was entitled to. Soon thereafter a disgusted Bounds ended his decades long career with the Department by resigning. The Department had become polluted by Windom's influence and the Riley administration, and Bounds would have no part of it. The charges by the Department were ridiculous, but they had their intended effect. Carriers began questioning Goff's integrity and moving their business to other insurers. In the end the Insurance Department had to drop fifty-nine of the sixty charges. John conceded to a single count of not having answered a correspondence from the Insurance Department within the ten days as required by regulations. He paid a fine and entered into an agreement with the Department that settled the matter with no further prosecution. But it would never be the same for John. He had to struggle everyday just to keep the company's doors open. The company was wounded and in a downward spiral.

Major Alabama newspapers carried the story of the extortion attempt. Of course it was big news, but it was not John's wish to turn it into a major scandal. In fact John thought he had an understanding with Gallion that this information would not be publicized, as it would do John and the Goff Group no good to take the story public. But Gallion contacted the news media, or had them contacted, and let the story out. To John, Gallion made it sound like he was incensed and outraged at this indignity. He was going to file suit against Bell, Windom, Price, Patrick, and the Alabama State Insurance Department. Gallion said he would take the case on contingency basis and John would have no out of pocket expense. Reluctantly John agreed and allowed the suit to be filed. Shortly thereafter Commissioner Bell resigned before being deposed.

John now believes that any action taken by Gallion on his behalf was for the benefit of Milton McGregor. Gallion's next move was to convince John to add the governor's name to the suit. While John was reluctant to do this, Gallion was insistent. Gallion had placed all of John's problems at Riley's feet, and finally John relented and allowed the governor's name to be included as a defendant. By adding Riley's name to the suit, the governor would be forced to testify, and that would win John's case and bring down the corrupt Riley administration. This was the biggest scandal in Alabama politics in years. Newspapers all up and down the state carried the story of the Alabama insurance executive who claimed to have been extorted by agents of the government.

If Riley took the stand, Gallion could question him about the Abramoff contribution and, once the administration was unraveled, McGregor's gambling empire would be able to survive. Tommy Gallion had backed the governor into a corner. If the lawsuit went forward and Riley testified, he would be indicted, convicted, driven from office, and sent to prison. The same fate might have awaited Steve Windom, Walter Bell, Ferrell Patrick, Mike Marsh, Jim Tait, and Don Price.

At a point in the battle Bob Riley's son, Rob, an attorney from Birmingham, called John at his home and implored him to drop the suit. John was unmoved. Shortly after taking office, Riley, now the top Republican in the state, helped Bill Canary to secure the presidency of the Business Council of Alabama, an association of several thousand members whose purpose was to promote the commercial interests of its members. Of this John says, "When you control the BCA, you control the biggest lobbying force in the state." The governor was in the pocket of Bill Canary, and Canary's influence extended all the way to Washington. It was Canary who helped to broker the Choctaw Indian/Riley campaign deal. And it was Bill Canary's influence with Karl Rove and the Bush administration that paved the way for his wife, Leura Canary, to be named the U.S. Attorney for the Middle District of the State of Alabama, one of the highest judicial offices in the state. Bill and Leura Canary were the most politically powerful couple in the State.

Tom Gallion poked the wrong rattlesnake when he went after Bob Riley. The governor was not out of ammunition. Under no circumstance would the governor testify. To do so would be the undoing of numerous Alabamans including the governor, lieutenant governor, insurance commissioner Bell, Ferrell Patrick, lobbyist Windom, and many others. Jack Abramoff and republican kingmaker, Karl Rove, could be dragged into it.

But Tommy Gallion was not prepared for what came next. He had misjudged Riley and Canary's influence, and they out-maneuvered him. In a court hearing related to the Goff versus the Insurance Department et al. civil suit, a startling prediction was made. In the court transcript of the case the judge used words to the effect, "I see what you guys are doing. You're going down to Leura Canary's office in Montgomery and get the U.S. Attorney to indict John Goff and make this whole thing go away." The statement was prophetic, because that's exactly what happened. U.S. Attorney Canary secured a grand jury indictment against John, and later brought charges against Milton McGregor and several other enemies of the governor, including state senators and representatives.

The headlines were dramatic. Insurance executive John Goff indicted! Not only had his good reputation been destroyed, but also now his freedom was at risk. At this point

John was still unaware of Tom Gallion's duplicitous role in this, and he continued to use him in his defense. From the U.S. Attorney's office the gloves came off. It was a bare-knuckle fight to save the governor and his allies. From the defense the effort was much less robust.

Prior to her appointment as a U.S. Attorney, Leura Canary's body of work as an attorney was uninspired. She was not strong and she was not considered particularly exceptional in legal circles. In fact, Mrs. Canary was very average, and her sole qualifications for her appointment as a federal prosecutor were that she had a law degree and she was married to Bill Canary. She was the perfect tool for the republican machine that was polluting Alabama politics. Indictments in Canary's territory were available for the asking when they came from the governor's office. When Riley wanted the popular ex-governor Don Siegelman indicted, it was Laura Canary who secured the indictment and conviction.

When Governor Riley needed to have John Goff silenced Laura Canary spent $5 million of the prosecutor's budget to fight him. In the indictments and trials of nine other threats to the governor, including Milton McGregor, Leura Canary spent $50 million to stage those trials. Her record in those efforts was zero for nine. Maybe convictions did not matter in these cases. Perhaps just the distraction of having to fight a criminal prosecution, and the expenditure of many millions of dollars for defense was enough to put the governor's enemies aside. Apropos this bullying tactic is the quote from the famous nineteenth century British Magistrate of History, Lord Acton: Absolute Power Corrupts Absolutely!

The conspiracy between the governor's office and the prosecutor had its intended effect. The civil case against Riley and the insurance department lost momentum. Haskell Slaughter and Tommy Gallion withdrew from the case, never notified John of this, and the statute of limitations for the case expired. John's resources were being rapidly depleted, and he had to focus what resources he had remaining on the criminal case. John was up against a motivated prosecutor who had the resources of the U.S. government at her disposal. Enemies of the governor were dealt with in the most notorious abuse of power in the history of Alabama politics.

In the indictment John was charged with embezzlement, mail fraud, and conspiracy. In the two-week trial Leura Canary recused herself, but made the notation that she wanted to be kept informed of all the proceedings related to it. Her replacement was A.U.S.A Steven Feaga, a fierce enemy of Tommy Gallion. Gallion's pretrial performance as John's defense counsel was weak. At a point in the trial Gallion withdrew as defense counsel, he said because he felt he could be of more assistance as a witness. With this turn of events A.U.S.A. Feaga threatened to Mirandize Gallion and charge him as a co-conspirator. Gallion left the courtroom and was whisked away to Florida in Milton McGregor's jet and, to protect himself, stayed away from Alabama for the duration of the trial. This left John in a bind because he was relying on Gallion to testify that John's actions with respect to the charges were done under advice of counsel. The job of defending John fell to Don Jones, a solo practitioner from Montgomery, and a hopeless alcoholic. Haskell Slaughter replaced Gallion with Jeremy Walker, a new lawyer who had just graduated from law school and had never tried a case. None of John's defense lawyers had any experience in federal criminal law, leaving John unarmed against the forces of the federal prosecutor's office. It spelled the end of John's legal defense.

The prosecutor made false claims about John's lifestyle and riches. That John owned a jet was true. But the claim that John had a collection of 1,500 ties, and a special room in his home just for his tie collection was an outrageous lie. But Don Jones did not object. Many other lies that the prosecutor told went unchallenged. The jury heard the most incredible things about John and his lifestyle, and his counsel rarely objected. Uncontested testimony that the jury heard would have spelled the end of anyone regardless of the truth or the good works that individual had ever performed. John had fifty witnesses, including his C.P.A. of twenty years, available to testify in his behalf. Jones only called one.

John was abandoned and deceived by his attorneys, Haskell Slaughter, Don Jones, and his long time friend and confidant Tommy Gallion. He never stood a chance. "If I could have testified I could have refuted all the charges, but my lawyers urged me not to do that," says John. "I would have been better off with a public defender."

In the end the jury returned a guilty verdict on charges of embezzlement, mail fraud, and filing a false statement with the insurance department. The embezzlement charge stemmed from a civil complaint relating to insurance premiums that one of the Goff Group's carriers claimed had been improperly withheld. Among John's explanations was that premiums payable to the the administrator for the carrier ECS had been overpaid, and any money due ECS or its carrier, XL/Greenwich, were kept in an account that ECS had access to. ECS by its own admission, had not reconciled the account, and could not say for certain that it had not received the premium payments it said it was owed. That matter had been settled by arbitration years earlier.

The charge that John had made a false statement to a state regulator involved a clerical error on an application form. In a brief filed by John's attorneys the defense stated, "The application does not contain any numerical data, financial representations, or calculations of any kind. Applicants are not asked to provide trust calculations, net worth, or asset valuations. Applicants are not asked to provide a financial statement. Since the false statement was not made in connection with a financial report or document, there is no violation of the law." Under normal circumstances, in the absence of political pressure, the State would simply contact a company and ask it to resubmit the document with the correct information. The overriding argument was that the filing of this documentation was a matter to be determined by the state of Alabama Department of Insurance, and not an issue for the federal prosecutors to argue. The prosecution was grasping at straws to find any charges with which to charge John. They seized and investigated 700,000 documents spanning John's entire career in an effort to come up with something.

John was convicted and sentenced to twelve years in prison, nearly a life sentence for a man his age. At his sentencing the judge suggested that in the trial there were a lot of actions that should be reviewed and could be reversed, and that the defense should work hard on the appeal. That appeal was filed with the 11th Circuit Court in Atlanta, but was denied. Subsequently John filed a motion to vacate his conviction based upon Ineffective Assistance of Counsel, but that motion was also denied.

Jim Ridling replaced Walter Bell as Insurance Commissioner when the whole case blew up. John ran into Ridling on the street one day and, in front of witnesses, was told, "If you had never sued Riley, none of this would ever have happened."

In the ruining of John Goff and his company, many others were made to suffer. His great regret is that the pressure of it all ruined his fifteen-year marriage to his wife Anne, and they divorced during this time. An organization like the Goff Group was a support system for many other people. Nationwide the company employed 280 people. That represented 280 families that had job security, employee benefits such as paid vacations and holidays, life and health insurance, matching 401K plans for retirement. Being in the employee benefit business, John made certain his own loyal employees always had the best. The company had a payroll of, and its employees paid payroll taxes on, $20 million per year. It purchased goods and services throughout the community in twice that amount. For Montgomery, a city of only about 200,000, that's a substantial impact. The Goff Group and John personally supported other charities such as the American Red Cross, where John was on the Board and spearheaded the effort to raise funds for its Montgomery headquarters building; youth soccer, football, and basketball leagues; the Museum of Fine Arts; the Shakespeare Festival; the Vintage Affair of the American Cancer Society. John was also a member of the Montgomery Committee of 100. And that's the shame of it all. A few politicians and their sycophants with self-serving agendas ruined all that, took down an entire socio-economic system that supported worthy employees and the community. Now Bob Riley has moved on to be a lobbyist as are Bill Canary and Ferrell Patrick, while John waited in prison for his eventual release.

After eight years of incarceration, John was released from FPC Pensacola in 2019 and sent to home confinement to serve out the rest of his sentence. The complete story, with all the details, is further memorialized in the full-length non-fiction book entitled *Johnny Dollar*.

The Caged Cajun
The Story of Howard Ronald Guillory

Howard "Ron" Guillory never sold or took drugs in his life, but that didn't stop prosecutors from charging him with conspiracy to distribute crack cocaine. He was not remotely involved in the event that led to this charge and yet he was convicted and given a ten-year prison sentence under the mandatory minimum sentencing guidelines.

Ron was born in 1954 in Oppaloussa, Louisiana. He was the second oldest of ten children, born to a father who was a truck driver and a mother who tried to earn a living as a housekeeper. He had that easy-going singsong demeanor and voice of a Louisiana Cajun. Ron worked hard all his life, quit school in the 11th grade to start work and help support his family. He is a blue-collar kind of guy who started out driving a truck and later owned an automobile paint and body shop in Lake Charles. He operated that business for twenty-four years and made a decent enough living to raise twelve children. When he divorced his first wife he was awarded custody of their eight children, and then helped raise the four children of his second wife brought from her failed first marriage. He always felt blessed to have such a fine family and a business that could support it. He was a content man with a lifestyle that included a family-first philosophy, and Christian beliefs to guide his life.

Ron's eldest son was named after his father. He was Howard, Jr. Junior was single, a motorcycle enthusiast, and a self-employed crack cocaine dealer. He lived in a trailer park in Lake Charles where his uncle, James LeBlanc, was a permanent houseguest. LeBlanc had been living with Junior for the past five years, and had lived with Ron for seven years before that. He was also employed at Ron's body shop. So, for a twelve-year period, Ron and his son gave LeBlanc a place to stay and a way to make a living. LeBlanc owed everything he had and was to these two men.

One day while Junior was convalescing in the hospital from a motorcycle accident, Ron received a telephone call from LeBlanc to see if he wanted to pick him up to go to a Wendy's restaurant for lunch. Ron said he could not because he was in the middle of a paint job and could not be interrupted. LeBlanc said he could wait. So it was arranged that Ron would pick up LeBlanc in the early afternoon and they would get lunch together. What Ron did not know at the time was that Junior had made a drug sale and was using LeBlanc to make the delivery.

Whitman Guillory (same last name but no relation to Ron) was a drug dealer and habitual user who had been arrested several times in the past on drug charges. Junior was one of his suppliers. The FBI had information on Whitman and was threatening him with a lengthy jail sentence unless he assisted in trapping a bigger supplier. Whitman placed Junior in his sights.

When Ron and LeBlanc arrived at the Wendy's, Whitman was waiting to make the buy. This came as a surprise to Ron, as he had no idea this was anything more than a quick lunch with his cousin. The FBI had wired Whitman up and gave him $1,700 to make the drug buy. Disappointed, but feeling there was nothing more to be done, Ron waited while LeBlanc made the sale of thirty-seven grams of crack.

In time Junior recovered from his motorcycle accident and was released from the hospital. He returned to his distribution business. Five years later, on June 2, 2002 tragedy struck the Guillory family. Junior was involved in a motorcycle accident; but this one resulted in his death. Despondent over Junior's death, the family thought things could not possibly get any worse. But it was wrong.

On October 12, 2006, in front of his wife and daughter, a dozen state police, and FBI agents in SWAT uniforms, descended upon Ron's body shop with search warrants for the business and for the home of Ron's seventy-five year old mother. Drug dogs and police officers combed through the business and found nothing of a criminal nature. On account of the business being clean of any illegal drugs, Ron was able to convince the police to abort their search of his mother's house. He had never been involved in the drug business, and certainly never had his mother.

Ron was taken in handcuffs to the Calcasieu Correctional Center (CCC) where he was charged with conspiracy to distribute more than fifty grams of crack cocaine. This is an important point because fifty grams carries with it a minimum mandatory sentence of ten years in prison. With the full knowledge that the FBI's purchase was thirty-seven grams, and with that being the actual amount negotiated between Whitman and LeBlanc, the prosecutor chose to file these false charges. The following day Ron appeared before the magistrate and was released on his own recognizance. Being a man of modest means, Ron did not have the $15,000 that an attorney would want to represent him. Under the circumstances the court appointed Brian Gill to defend him. The arrest was a result of a drug transaction that took place five years earlier in which James LeBlanc delivered drugs to Whitman Guillory. In order to lessen their penalties both men lied in their testimony and said that Ron was part of the conspiracy.

Not surprisingly, the arrest warrant on Ron's case was issued twenty days prior to the expiration of the statue of limitations. In this instance the assumption that justice is swift, and dangerous criminals are removed from society in order to make our communities safe, was an illusion. But Junior was a known drug dealer who was distributing drugs before the event at Wendy's, and most likely during the five-year period that followed. He was only stopped from delivering drugs because of his death. Law enforcement failed to protect society against a known dealer, and then indicted his father, who had nothing to do with the crime, and had never been a threat to society.

A real drug dealer might be offered better options when facing charges than an innocent man. The real drug dealer has handled the drugs and has sold or delivered them. More important, the real drug dealer has purchased the drugs from a bigger distributor. He has information about other distributors, so a prosecutor can go after bigger suppliers. An innocent man like Ron has no bargaining chip because he doesn't travel in those distribution circles. He doesn't know anybody. There is no one for him to give up. And that is a big part of the reason James LeBlanc was offered a plea deal and Ron was not. When the indictment came down, Ron was charged with two counts: conspiracy to sell drugs, and trafficking in drugs. LeBlanc not only had four charges against him, he also had an enhancement having had previous arrests and convictions. He could have been facing twenty years in prison if he didn't give investigators a good story.

Prior to his trial Ron believed that Brian Gill, his court appointed attorney, would be able to give him adequate representation. Gill seemed interested in the case and even came to the body shop to see what he could learn about Ron's lifestyle and character. He instilled confidence in Ron. He told Ron that his case was winnable and that the government had nothing on him that would lead to a conviction. But, when it came to the trial, Ron was sadly disappointed. He was disappointed that Gill gave such a bad impression to the court. Gill slouched in his chair. He did not stand to address the court and the jury as is customary in U.S. courts. And he did not make the proper objections to testimony that was given by Ron's accusers. His accusers turned out to be not only prosecutor Bret Grayson, but also his own cousin, James LeBlanc. (LeBlanc had been offered a plea bargain, but when questioned by the judge at his plea conference, he began to go into a long, unbelievable explanation about his being a victim of Junior. The judge, Patricia Minaldi, rejected the plea offer and required LeBlanc to stand trial.) In order to try to lessen the sentence that was going to be proposed, LeBlanc attempted to appease the prosecution, the judge, and the jury. He testified that Ron knew about the drug deal at the Wendy's restaurant. He also testified that he was forced to sell drugs for Junior under threat of being evicted from his house. LeBlanc was a crack addict himself, and it was Ron's belief that he gladly sold and delivered drugs in order to support his own habit.

Even before he testified, Brian Gill had an opportunity to have the case against Ron dismissed. On the opening day of the trial, after the jury selection was complete, the testimony against Ron began. Gill requested permission to approach the bench. LeBlanc's attorney, Michael McHale, along with Gill and U.S. Attorney Brett Grayson, assembled in front of Judge Minaldi's bench. Gill made a motion to have the charges against Ron dropped for lack of evidence. The judge was actually impressed, and her preliminary thought was to grant the motion. That could have been the end of it, and Ron could have gone home a free and innocent man. In fact the judge said that there was a good case for an acquittal, and had Gill made the motion to dismiss the charges before testimony began, she probably would have granted it. However, instead of doing the right thing for an innocent man before the justice system, Judge Minaldi ruled that because the jury had already begun hearing testimony, the trial against Ron could continue.

The trial lasted for three days. Ron could only watch as Brian Gill made a miserable showing while Michael McHale made a spectacular case for LeBlanc. At one point in the trial McHale leaned over to Gill and said, "They don't have anything on your client."

After three days of testimony the case was given over to the jury to decide. During deliberation the jury foreman sent a note to the judge asking to see the indictment because, based on the testimony, it could not find sufficient evidence to convict Ron. The proper thing for the judge at that point would have been for her to instruct the jury to return a verdict based upon the evidence. But that is not what Judge Minaldi did. What she did was to provide a copy of the indictment to the jury. (She said it was because it was public information.) Of this Ron said, "After that I never had a chance. The indictment, as many do in other cases, made me look like Al Capone." When questioned about this, Ron understands that indictments are accusations, and prosecutors can say just about anything they want to convince a grand jury to issue an indictment with little or no evidence being presented against the accused. Of his accuser, U.S. Attorney Bret Grayson, Ron is clear and succinct in his description. "He's a real piece of shit," said Ron. He was seldom known to swear.

The jury returned a guilty verdict against both Ron and LeBlanc. Both men were given ten-year prison sentences. James LeBlanc, because he was guilty; Ron Guillory because LeBlanc lied about him, and because Judge Minaldi allowed tainted testimony against him. And because Bret Grayson had no conscience about prosecuting an innocent man; and because his attorney was ineffective and incompetent in his defense.

Years later Ron sat in jail, his life in tatters. The body shop that supported his family and his extended family for twenty-four years is closed. His family misses its husband, father, brother, grandfather. His wife has taken a second job to try to meet her bills. And as an ironic aside, Judge Minaldi later had to face DUI charges in a traffic accident.

Ask a hundred convicts what they were charged with and most of them will say conspiracy. Conspiracy is a catchall term that gives prosecutors free reign to go after individuals who may or may not have been involved in a crime, no matter how far removed from the actual event they may have been at the time it occurred. Ask the average inmate in federal prison and he might say that if the shoe were on the other foot, it is the criminal justice system that is involved in conspiracy – conspiracy to incarcerate people, to keep jails full, to feed the prison machine from which so much money is derived. It takes a special kind of uncaring, mean, and vindictive individual to participate in this corruption of America's criminal justice system.

Author's note: In the Federal Prison Camp (FPC) Pensacola we called Ron 'Mr. Howard.' He was friendly with everybody everyday, and he was one of the most popular inmates in the camp. He and I could not have been much different, but we were great friends, very fond of each other. Mr. Howard developed problems in his colon area that he reported to the medical personnel. Without examining him they diagnosed it as hemorrhoids. For months Mr. Howard would go over to the clinic as his conditions continued to worsen. He told me of his unbearable pain and bleeding from his rectum. When he awoke in the mornings his bed would be covered in blood. He had gotten to the point where he could not walk and had to move around in a wheel chair. Finally, after Mr. Howard complained for more than eighteen months, the medical staff sent him see an outside specialist. He was thoroughly examined and biopsies were taken on two tumors each the size of a grapefruit. How the medical staff at the camp didn't see that is a mystery. The specialist hung his head and told Mr. Howard that if he had come in six months earlier he could possibly have done something to help him. But now his condition was too far advanced to do anything about it. Mr. Howard was given only a few months to live. As is the rule in circumstances where an inmate's condition is beyond the capabilities of the camp medical staff, he was transferred to the Federal Medical Center (FMC) in Butner, NC. There he died on April 4, 2016. An innocent man, charged, convicted, incarcerated and allowed to die through neglect and incompetence of the criminal justice system.

I attended a small memorial for Mr. Howard that was performed in the chapel at FPC Pensacola. It was a somber moment and many of his friends attended. But, when James LeBlanc got up to speak, I never came so close to getting myself in trouble with the camp guards. I wanted to grab him by the throat and choke the life out of him. My stomach reacted every time I saw that slimy little bastard in the camp.

International Injustice
The Michael Balboa Story

The collapse of investment bank Lehman Brothers in September of 2008 ushered in a banking crisis of proportions never imagined. The signs of trouble had been apparent for several years. A decade of excess credit spawned a real estate bubble not only in America's residential communities, but also in commercial and residential markets throughout the world. Within weeks of the Lehman collapse the two largest financial organizations in the world, the multi-trillion-dollar private companies, Fannie Mae and Freddie Mac, were declared insolvent, and were placed in conservatorship under the protection of the United States Treasury. For the first time in history private debt had to be guaranteed by the U.S. government in order to avoid a default with a resulting worldwide economic depression. With no banking system, and no credit the planet would be cast into utter chaos. Without a government bailout of the U.S. banking system it would have been the end of the world as we knew it.

Bank regulators painted many banks with the same brush. The Office of the Comptroller of the Currency (OCC) regulated the U.S. banks. The Security and Exchange Commission (SEC) had authority over all public corporations, including foreign banks doing business in the U.S. With brutal force these two regulatory agencies set about to punish all but the most conservative of lenders. This left a target-rich environment for enforcement. Heads would roll and credit markets would never be the same.

With loan defaults rising and pressure from regulators, banks began to take a closer look at their investment portfolios. Soon consumer credit became scarce. Commercial loans and credit lines were not renewed. Many small businesses that relied on credit were forced out of business. In a single year 300 of largest and most reliable mortgage lenders in the country imploded. Home loans dried up and the commercial and residential real estate markets, including what had heretofore been a healthy construction industry, ground to a halt. Major economies around the world went into a recession affecting everyone in one way or another.

It wouldn't take long before the portfolio managers, who had produced excellent year after year results for their investors through sophisticated investment strategies, would be affected by the worldwide credit crunch. Hedge funds, which perform extensive market research and frequently invest in obscure, non-traditional investments, including the use of synthetic derivatives to hedge their positions, operate in a world that may appear foreign to less knowledgeable investors. This includes a general lack of understanding by bankers and regulators. Succinctly put, banks were lending against investments of which they had little understanding. And it did not matter how successfully the portfolios had performed. If the banker did not understand the investment, or if the securities within the portfolio were illiquid and difficult to value, the portfolio manager's credit lines were in jeopardy.

Millennium Global Emerging Credit Fund was just such a hedge fund. The term "emerging markets" applies to those countries whose offerings, whether they be in the form of sovereign debt or shares of public companies, carry a financial stature below that of better recognized and understood economies and currencies of such countries as the United States, Germany, and Canada. Emerging markets are derived from all of the countries of Africa, South and Central America, the Caribbean, Eastern Europe, the Middle Eastern countries, and all of Asia with the exception of Japan and South Korea. Interest in investing in these emerging countries is generated when the subject country demonstrates that it has a relatively educated work force, a stable government and currency, and the infrastructure that allows for its producers to bring their goods to the worldwide markets. A portfolio manager who specializes in the debt of emerging economies has his finger on the pulse of these countries, knows their politics, GDP, currency and banking, and sees wherein the opportunity lies for investing in their securities and sovereign debt. This was the profile of Michael Balboa, the portfolio manager for this particular Millennium Fund. And the results he produced for Millennium investors was an impressive 30% year over year for the period 2005 to 2008.

Mike Balboa received his college degree with high honors from Hofstra University in 1991. As an undergraduate Mike wrote two articles that were published in respectable journals. His study on the transition of the Russian government from a communist economy to a capitalist economy, and its effect on the ruble, gave insight into Mike's understanding of international currencies. This article was published in the Journal of Developmental Economics. His article on NASADQ phase-in stocks and market inefficiencies showed insight into market dynamics far beyond the undergraduate level, and was published in the Journal of Finance. He began studies for an MBA degree at NYU's Stern College, but quit the program when he felt insulted by the curriculum requirement that he take an entry-level finance course. Taking a course that he could have taught was a waste of his time.

The research department at Wall Street house Solomon Brothers took note of these articles and was impressed with the fact that Mike not only understood international currencies and market dynamics, but could also write about it. They hired him to do research for them in the area of emerging markets.

After four years at Solomon, where he was mostly doing research, and not as much trading as he would have liked, he saw an opportunity at the emerging markets fund of Strategos. In this place he was able to rebalance his responsibilities and concentrate on analysis and trading. Being a trader gave Mike the freedom he needed to perform at a higher level. He worked at Strategos from 1995 to 1999. It was during this time that he married his British born wife Andria. When an offer came from Greenwich Europe Emerging Markets to join them in London doing research and trading, and understanding that it was his new wife's desire to return home, Mike grabbed the opportunity, and the family relocated. In 2001 a client of Mike's, Rainbow Global High Yield Fund, a hedge fund operated by a very wealthy Frenchman living in Monaco, wanted to reenergize his own fund with Mike as its manager. Mike had produced startling results for Rainbow in a trade involving the sovereign debt of Bosnia, and this fund wanted Mike all to itself. Over a five-year period Mike grew the organization from $25 million in assets to $250 million in assets. He was becoming a rock star in the emerging markets scene, and making a lot of money for his clients.

In 2006 Mike was given an opportunity to realize a dream. He had friends at Millennium Global Investments who had invested in Rainbow and liked the results Mike had produced for them. They wanted to start a new fund with Mike as its portfolio manager. Millennium Global Emerging Markets Credit Fund was born. Hedge funds operate much differently from mutual funds in several aspects. Mutual funds invest the money of their clients, taking long positions in stocks, bonds, futures contracts, and options for a set annual percentage fee regardless of their performance. Hedge funds use equity provided by investors to purchase and structure securities, but they also use that equity to leverage debt (borrow from investors to increase their size). They also take short positions and create derivatives. As opposed to a small fee for managing others' investments, their compensation comes in the form of a percentage, usually around 20% of the profits they return. Hedge funds often do not sell shares on a retail basis; their investors are more frequently institutional with multi-billion dollar net worths. They have teams of investment analysts, and their normal minimum investment could be in the hundreds of thousands or millions of dollars.

This new fund started out modestly with an investment of $20 million from the parent fund. But Mike had a strong following and within a year had brought in about $120 million from former clients. Millennium was also provided credit lines from banks throughout the world. The terms of these credit lines were dependent upon specific bank's matching equity requirements, including the nature of the investments within the fund, taking into consideration the credit quality and liquidity of the underlying collateral. Advances against these credit lines were made pursuant to the banks' examination and evaluation of the portfolio as a whole. None of the lenders had the staff capabilities of evaluating each specific trade or position and there was simply too much activity including equity positions, synthetic investments, and hedges, to follow what was going on. Mike, as portfolio manager, knew every position and its hedge, and knew exactly how and when to trade into or out of a position. It was a dynamic market that required a great deal of sophistication to understand. The banks rarely knew or understood the value of their collateral in spite of the fact that Mike kept a continuous flow of information about the portfolio going to them.

Valuations were updated constantly and published monthly. The Millennium Emerging Markets Credit Fund was the only one of Millennium's funds to use the services of Globe Op. That company is the worldwide leader in asset valuation for its clients. They have the best modeling software and state of the art reporting services of value to institutional investors such as hedge funds. Mike always felt that this third party check provided independent testimony as to the integrity of its asset valuations. Aside from consulting with Mike and his analysts as to their valuation methodology, Globe Op also checked with counter-parties on trades to see if the information they used in creating the trade was in alignment with their own facts and the information provided by the Millennium analysts. It is not unusual for the value of an asset within a fund to fluctuate by as much as 3% or more in a month. For this reason values are constantly being revised and updated.

For several years bankers had been exposed to risks in the Credit Default Swap (CDS) markets. Collateralized Mortgage Obligations (CMO) had already begun to default as a result of the sub-prime crisis. Banks throughout the world had been buying U.S. mortgage debt and were feeling the pain of non-performance by their counter-parties. Unable to fund their own obligations, many of the largest banks in the world exited the overnight interbank market. If the banks could not keep abreast of their own funding obligations, they certainly could not be in a position to use excess funds, of which there were none, to fund the needs of others. Overnight interbank credit dried up, and many of the banks had to look to the collateral of their borrowers for liquidity. They would force their borrowers to pay off, or pay down, their loans and lines of credit.

While things were going well, they went very well. But that was soon to change. By 2008 the fund Mike was managing had grown to $4 billion, comprised of $1 billion in equity and $3 billion in debt. Credit Swiss was the main funding source. Lenders with lesser interests in Millennium debt included Citi Group, UBS, Morgan Stanley, J P Morgan, and Barclays Bank. Unable to fund its own balance sheet, and with no interbank cooperation, Credit Swiss changed its methodology from portfolio funding, that is lending against the fund's entire pool of assets, to asset specific funding. This meant they would mark to market each of the securities or positions within the fund, and require Millennium to either post additional collateral or pay down the line of credit. Millennium was given forty-eight hours to comply. But many of the investments in the fund were illiquid. They had credit default swaps and numerous other difficult to value types of investments. Even though these investments were performing, there was no organized secondary market for them, meaning Credit Swiss could take latitude in their valuation. What had one day been booked at one hundred cents on the dollar (an expression of value although many of these investments were not denominated in dollars) Credit Swiss slashed the implied value of the underlying securities to a fraction of their actual value. The requirement to pay down the credit line, or post additional collateral, effectively paralyzed Millennium, and in spite of Herculean efforts on the part of Millennium management, a default could not be avoided. Practically overnight Credit Swiss destroyed the hedge fund that Mike had worked to build, and that had made so much money for so many people. Credit Swiss' call triggered a default by Millennium, and the fund had no alternative but to seek protection from the courts in Bermuda, the country where the fund was registered.

It was left to the Bermuda Monetary Authority to oversee the wind down of the fund. KPMW was appointed liquidator. Each creditor was left with the responsibility to manage and liquidate the collateral it held, and KPMW forensics was to report to the Monetary Authority. In the end KPMW's report indicated that none of the banks, with the exception of Barclays Bank, was diligent in its efforts to acquire reasonable value for the securities it either marketed or took into portfolio. Barclays actually used its vast resources to sell these Millennium assets, and gave an accounting of its valuation and final results. It showed that it cared about market integrity and market prices. As a result, the losses in that part of the portfolio were minimized.

KPMW's report went on to criticize Credit Swiss as the lead bank, and the other participating banks for booking Millennium's assets at prices that had no relationship to their value. From a bookkeeping perspective, one day they wrote down the value to a fraction of what they were actually worth; the following day these same assets appeared on their books at a much higher value. Thus were destroyed $800 million of Millennium's investors' assets, and transferred to the books of Credit Swiss and the other creditors. A copy of this report was sent to all interested parties including investors in the fund, creditors of the fund, and officers of the fund. No one was ever prosecuted for this fraud against Millennium and its investors.

With the collapse of the Millennium Emerging Markets Credit Fund, and with epic disarray in the financial markets, Mike saw opportunity in the area of asset recovery for investors in Mortgage Backed Securities (MBS). With three partners he formed Asset Recovery Advisors and Managers, LLC (ARAM) with headquarters in London, and offices in New York and Singapore. This new company developed proprietary software that allowed them to run tapes on mortgage portfolios. Defaulted loans would be run through the modeling engine to look for flaws in the underwriting and/or servicing of loans by the originator, seller, or servicer. If discrepancies were discovered in the covenants between the investor and a holder in due course, the investor could "put back", meaning require the offending party to repurchase the loan, at par. In the multi-trillion dollar mortgage industry this process could save investors billions, or tens of billions of dollars. It was a sound business model, and it was state of the art in the mortgage industry. This appeared to be Mike's new career path.

In 2009 a fund from the U.S. called Pontifex filed suit against Millennium, its officers, and creditors. Pontifex had lost money on a small position it owned in Millennium's Emerging Markets Credit Fund. At the time Mike had no knowledge of any American investors in his fund. It had never marketed itself in the States and, while understanding that his investors came from all over the world, this was the first he had heard of any American investors. As a part of its posturing for a favorable settlement, Pontifex tried to apply pressure by filing a complaint with the SEC and providing them with a copy of the KPMW report. In 2009 Millennium received word that the SEC had opened its own investigation into the matter. The civil complaint of Pontifex was filed in New York, but was quickly disposed of in favor of Millennium. The court said the suit was frivolous. Pontifex appealed the court decision, but that appeal was also turned down for lack of merit. Two times the U.S. courts stood by the innocence of the Millennium defendants.

In February of 2010, pursuant to the receipt of the KPMW report, the Financial Services Authority (FSA) initiated an investigation of the Millennium Fund. The FSA is the British equivalent of America's SEC, and has regulatory authority over public offerings and financial affairs in that country. Since Millennium operated out of London, the FSA was the appropriate regulator for this matter. KPMW forensics detailed, position-by-position, each of the assets in the fund. They checked Mike's valuation models against their own methodologies and found them to be safe, sound, and reasonable in their assumptions. The study exonerated Mike and senior management from any wrongdoing. It also pointed out the creditors' irresponsible handling of the default. For six months the FSA studied the report, formulated its own assessment of the assets and their disposition, reviewed Millennium's methodology for valuation, and conducted interviews. Over a period of five weeks, for several days per week, eight to ten hours a day, Mike met with FSA's investigators. They discussed the underlying securities, the valuation, Millennium's marketing and back office procedures, and the treatment by the creditors. The investigation was thorough and fair. In the end Mike and Millennium were given a clean bill of health. It was decided that they had done nothing wrong.

By 2011 it appeared that the pain of the Millennium failure was in Mike's rear view mirror. Hundreds of nagging problems with investors had been cleared up. The KPMW report was completed, and the conclusion favored the Millennium officers and directors. The government of Bermuda was satisfied. The FSA had concluded that no one at the fund had done anything illegal or inappropriate. The New York appeals court had thrown out the Pontifex matter, and no one had heard anything from the SEC. It appeared that all matters related to the collapse of the Millennium Emerging Markets Credit Fund had been settled.

In November of that year Mike traveled to New York to have meetings with investors who wanted to buy into some of his deals. It was a perfect opportunity to visit his parents who still lived in New York, and to do some Christmas shopping for his wife and three young children. On the night of November 30th he was alone, staying at the tony Mondrian Hotel in Soho. He had been out late with colleagues and did not get to sleep until after midnight. At 4:00 a.m. Mike was awakened by a loud banging on the door to his hotel room. He arose from a deep sleep and opened the door to see what the commotion was about. There he was confronted by two men who introduced themselves as agents of the U.S. Postal Inspector Service. They asked if he was Michael Balboa of Millennium. He answered in the affirmative. He was advised there was a warrant for his arrest. He was given five minutes to get dressed, pack, and check out. He was being taken into custody. At the time, Mike was not unaware of any investigation or warrants, nor was he told what the charges were, only that it was related to Millennium. For the first few minutes of this episode Mike thought he was dreaming. But he soon learned that this nightmare was no illusion.

After his intake at the Detention Center under the Manhattan Court House, Mike was given the opportunity to make a telephone call. Not being connected to anyone in New York who could help him, he called his attorney in London. From that conversation the wheels started turning. Through its connections, the law firm came up with the name of Joe Tacopina as the best choice to handle Mike's defense. Tacopina is a highly regarded criminal defense attorney of the stature of perhaps Melvin Belli, Alan Dershowitz, or Roy Black. He's tough, he's smart, and he wins cases. This was bad news for the prosecution. He swung into action for his new client. When he asked the prosecutor what the charges were, he was told that Mike was being held on a complaint, not an indictment. This was a rare use of prosecutorial authority.

A day later Mike's parents posted a $5 million bond to have him released. Mike surrendered his passport and the judge placed him under house arrest with an ankle monitor, and released him to the home of his parents, not far away in Melville, Long Island. Joe Tacopina was incessant in his demand that the prosecutor either charge his client or release him. With the public notice of Mike's arrest there had been scores of articles in such widely circulated periodicals as the Wall Street Journal, the Times of London, Business Week, Reuters, and Bloomberg. By the time Associated Press got hold of the story, the publicity surrounding the case had gone viral. Every financial journal in the world wanted to carry the story of this hedge fund manager's plight. And this publicity played right into the hands of the very ambitious prosecutor Preet Bharara. Bharara was the U.S. Attorney from the Southern District of New York, and it was his name on the complaint in the matter of the United States of America versus Michael Balboa. At this time the U.S. Attorney General, Eric Holder, was on the hot seat in Washington, and it was widely rumored that President Obama was looking for his replacement. Political observers postulated that Bharara was looking for headlines and posturing for the Attorney General position. Bharara had routinely been criticized for being soft on U.S. bankers in the wake of the 2008 financial meltdown. He needed some notches in his bedpost without offending the local banking elite. The Balboa case might just be the ticket to fulfill that ambition by showing the public, and the President, that he had international influence in the criminal justice system. During the course of the investigation Bharara issued four press releases related to the case. In this unusual move, he wanted to show the public that he was tough on these Wall Street types. Curiously, Mike and Millennium were not from Wall Street, they were from London.

Three months following Mike's arrest, an indictment was handed down by the New York Grand Jury. Mike was charged with single counts of securities fraud, wire fraud, investment advisor fraud, and conspiracy to commit securities and wire fraud. The prosecutor contended that it is illegal for the portfolio manager to be involved in the valuation of the securities within the portfolio, and that investors "were never told that he would be involved in the valuation process." It ignored the fact that Mike had no input into the offering information provided by Millennium. Mike was the portfolio manager; he was the rainmaker, creating positions, executing trades, and raking in the profits. The offering information on his fund was the domain of the Millennium marketing department.

In the negotiations between attorney Tacopina and Assistant U.S. Attorney Chris Levine, the prosecutor tried dozens of times to have Mike agree to a plea bargain. The prosecution's best offer was to have Mike plead to a single count of conspiracy to commit securities fraud and receive a five year prison sentence. Tacopina, with years of experience in such matters, had never seen a prosecutor try so many times to arrive at a plea bargain. He told Mike that this was the behavior of a prosecutor who had little faith in the outcome, and was trying to save face with a minor conviction. Mike wasn't going for it because he felt he was on solid ground. He offered to plead guilty to nothing more than a parking ticket to have the matter disposed of.

A year later the trial commenced in the Manhattan Federal Court, and the publicity started again. The matter at hand revolved around the valuation of a single asset within the portfolio on which Globe Op and Mike had given an opinion of value that was in dispute. In the early 1990s the African nation of Nigeria was in dire financial trouble. It restructured its debt through the issuance of Brady Bonds. This offering carried warrants representing a general obligation of the country that Mike believed were selling at a deep discount. Since the economy of Nigeria is dependent in large part on oil production, as the price of oil moved, so moved the value of the warrants. At the time the warrants were issued, oil was less than $40 per barrel. A decade later, when oil topped $120 per barrel, the market value for the warrants would logically become worth more. Those warrants held by his fund were valued accordingly. In a portfolio with assets in excess of $4 billion, a portfolio that had performed well and brought outstanding returns to its investors, the United States contended that Mike had broken the law when he rendered an opinion of value of the Nigerian warrants. In fact the offering information related to the fund specifically disclosed that the portfolio manager would render opinions of value of securities within the fund. The asset that was in question was the Nigerian warrants, a $60 million position that represented only 1.5% of the portfolio. But the prosecutor's ego and zeal were not to be denied.

With Millennium's presence and reputation, it was motivated to distance itself from Mike, to paint him as a rogue trader, and to place the blame for the negative publicity surrounding the collapse of its hedge fund on him. Mike's defense was that he was at all times forthcoming and open about the assets in the portfolio. He had no reason to exaggerate values, and he had substantial backup for his methodology including the independent opinions of Globe Op. The counter-party on the Nigerian warrants was Gilles Descharsonville. The information he gave to Globe Op supported Mike's conclusion of value.

At trial the prosecution's first witness was Maria Gibson Stark, the compliance officer for Millennium. Ms. Gibson Stark was the responsible party within the Millennium organization who signed off on offering brochures, due diligence questionnaires, and such other kinds of published documentation that might brush up against the law in the course of business. She was also the human resource compliance officer. The nature of her testimony centered around such subjects as Mike's compensation, a tactic that frequently has the effect of prejudicing the jury. On that issue she discussed Mike's total compensation in such a way as to imply everything he earned came from an overvalued asset. In fact, Mike's management compensation for the Nigerian debt holdings were a minuscule part of his overall pay check. Ms. Gibson Stark claimed that she knew nothing of Mike's activities, and that Mike acted alone and kept the parent company in the dark. All telephone conversations within the company were recorded, and it would have been helpful to the defense if this witness would have produced them. But the company conveniently lost the tapes. The court had to rely on Ms. Gibson Stark's word, but with no backup for her accusations. The company did however produce some of Mike's emails, but Mike believes that some of them had been purged. Ms. Gibson Stark was barred from discussing the FSA report that had exonerated Mike several years earlier.

The prosecution's next key witness was Gilles Descharsonville, the counter-party on those Nigerian warrants, the securities in question. Over the course of three years Mr. Descharsonville had given sworn testimony to the FSA, the SEC, and the Spanish securities regulators. For that whole time, and on each occasion, the story he told was consistent, and it fully supported Mike's case. But when the prosecutor threatened to indict him, followed by an offer of immunity, Descharsonville changed his story and gave testimony that incriminated Mike. The government contended that Mike and Descharsonville schemed to influence Globe Op into accepting an inflated value for the Nigerian warrants. It pressured Descharsonville into lying and saying that he and Mike had done this with the intent to mislead Globe Op and their customers. When he was done being questioned by the prosecution it was Joe Tacopina's chance to cross examine. The attorney reiterated several of the questions the prosecutor had asked where Descharsonville had answered the same questions when posed by either the FSA, the SEC, KPMW, or the Spanish regulators. The answers to these authorities and auditors were completely opposite the answers he had just given in response to the prosecutor's questions. He was asked if he had been given immunity for testifying against Mike. He answered that he had, provided that he told the truth. He was asked who would determine the truth. He answered that the jury would determine the truth. Mr. Tacopina produced a copy of the immunity agreement between the prosecutor and Mr. Descharsonville and asked him to read from page five, words to the affect, "The government shall decide what the truth is." Then he was asked if he had met with the prosecutor in advance of the testimony he was about to give, and for how long had they met. He answered that they spent two days going over the story the prosecutor was expecting to hear. Mr. Tacopina concluded that Mr. Descharsonville had given testimony on numerous occasions that led to Mike's exoneration, and then changed his story for the prosecutors in order to escape criminal charges of his own. Descharsonville tried to wiggle out of it by saying that he had lied to the regulators and auditors on previous occasions and he was telling the truth now.

After a three-week trial, the jury was charged with arriving at a verdict. Many complicated matters had been discussed in the trial and some of the details the jury was supposed to rule on would have taken a financial expert to fully understand. After nearly two weeks of deliberation the jury foreman emerged and told the court that it was simply incapable of grasping all of the intricacies of the financial transactions and valuations that had been presented. It was not a deadlocked jury; it was a jury that had the integrity and candor to say it could not do the job with which it had been charged. The judge declared a mistrial and Mike was free to go. For now the matter was closed, and if the prosecutor wanted to pursue the case he would have to ask for a retrial. The defeat for Preet Bharara was an embarrassment. This time he did not issue a press release.

In the five month period between the end of Mike's first trial in June 2013, and the beginning of his second trial in December 2013, the prosecution took a good look at what went wrong for it, and formulated a strategy against which defense was a challenge. In the first trial the government was trying to demonstrate that Mike had broken the law by being involved in the valuation of the fund's assets, particularly the Nigerian warrants. When that strategy failed, ending in a mistrial, it changed course and its efforts centered on trying to prove that the value of the warrants had been vastly overstated. In order to prove its case, it called a suspicious cast of characters to testify, all of whom had their own agenda, and all of whom stood to gain by being less than completely honest. And the judge went along with it. Pursuant to a pre-trial hearing the judge issued a Limitation Order in favor of the prosecution that tied the hands of the defense. In that Limitation Order the rules for the second trial all but guaranteed a victory for the prosecution.

When asked if there were any changes to the witness list, the prosecution indicated that they would like to add a few names and make some like-for-like substitutions.

Several names were given as additional witnesses. The defense believed these names were added as a distraction, meaning they would have to use resources to interview some of these people. But one substitution was anything but like-for-like. In the first trial a rather low level functionary of Citi Group had been called on to testify about the Nigerian warrants. This individual was responsible for the payments linked to the fiscal agency agreement related to the warrants. He was very close to the transaction and knew it thoroughly, and better still, he had no agenda with respect to any of the parties involved. He was neutral. His testimony was concise and accurate, and no damage to the defense. Now the prosecution asked that they be allowed to replace that witness with the man who was the Minister of Finance for Nigeria in 2006 and 2007, a time during which warrants were being redeemed by the country (but not the time frame within which Millennium had valued the warrants). Further, while the prosecution was able to lionize Minister Mansour Muhtar and bolster his reputation, the Limitation Order prohibited the defense from bringing out the fact that Minister Muhtar had been kicked out of office for corruption.

Each hedge fund publishes its AIMA (Alternative Investment Management Association) questionnaire. AIMA publishes guidelines related to the valuation of illiquid assets. Millennium's AIMA questionnaire specifically showed that the portfolio manager's involvement was appropriate. The judge would not allow the full text of the AIMA guidelines to be placed in evidence. This was detrimental to Mike's case as allowing the guidelines into evidence would have demonstrated the fund was following the proper guidelines, and would have added to Mike's credibility as a manager who was following the established rules.

Further, the judge granted the prosecution's request that any discussion of Mike's valuation of assets be limited to the Nigerian warrants. The jury would never hear about the many hundreds of valuations in which Mike had been involved about which there was no dispute.

As oil prices escalated, Nigeria had been banking huge amounts of money. It set up a fund the proceeds of which would go toward redeeming debt. In a memo Mike had prepared for Millennium's attorneys in the Pontifex matter, the subject of which was sovereign value recovery rights, he noted that the Nigerian fund was being used to buy back the warrants. It was from that activity that he got the notion that the warrants had value, and helped in making the decision to purchase them. The defense wanted to use that memo. It demonstrated that Mike was an expert in this field, having traded in the debt of such countries as Bosnia, Nigeria, Argentina, and Uruguay. The paper had information that clarified for the layman the methodology that went into valuing, and the decision to purchase certain kinds of sovereign debt. The enthusiasm of Millennium's investors was testament to its success. But that paper never saw the light of day with respect to Mike's defense. The prosecution had effectively gotten the judge to hone down the allowable evidence to such a degree that defending Mike became nearly impossible.

FinRA (Financial Regulatory Agency) is the successor regulator to the National Association of Securities Dealers (NASD), the agency that regulates broker/dealers. Their representative brought dozens of professionally prepared graphs and charts related to the hedge fund's assets. All of these exhibits exaggerated and distorted the size of the Nigerian warrants as a percentage of the overall portfolio. The witness gave a misleading picture as to the impact this particular asset had on the fund. It is said that statistics can be used, or misused, to paint any picture a person is trying to paint. This witness' testimony and exhibits stretched the limits of creativity while attempting to excoriate Mike. Of just as much concern is the unlikelihood that any of the jurors could understand this subterfuge.

Honesty was not Mansour Muhtar's long suit, having been scandalously forced from his office as the Nigerian Minister of Finance in a very public sacking over charges of corruption. In hopes of currying favor with the government, Minister Muhtar skewed his testimony in such a way as to make Mike look as bad as possible. He tried to discredit Mike's write-up related to the valuation of illiquid assets, particularly saying that there was no market for the warrants in question, that there was no collateral to back them up, and that they had no value. He went overboard in trying to impress his own government, while giving irresponsible testimony related to the warrants, none of which was based on facts.

The Human Resources and Compliance Officer for Millennium, Maria Gibson Stark, followed Millennium's corporate line of trying to lay as much blame as possible on Mike, and show him in the worst light possible. She went into great detail about Mike's salary for a specific reason. Mike was a very well paid portfolio manager, as would be any hedge fund manager who had worked in the industry for twenty years and produced an exceptional track record. Large salaries impress juries in a negative way. Ms. Gibson Stark's testimony made it look like Mike had over-valued the Nigerian warrants and banked a fortune from it. In fact Mike never earned any money at all on that asset.

When the defense took over, it did an admirable job of refuting the government's case by presenting witnesses and exhibits that supported the argument for Mike's innocence. After all, nothing the government offered in the way of testimony (or facts) proved its case for a conviction. Karoline Molberg, Millennium's marketing director, was an excellent defense witness. Ms. Molberg testified that she knew Mike well and was fully familiar with his work. It was Ms. Molberg who created the offering brochures for the Emerging Markets Credit Fund. She said that as far as she knew everything that Mike did with respect to running the fund, and providing information for the valuation of its assets, was done correctly.

The defense also called in several of the investors in the Millennium fund as witnesses. Each investor had fifteen to twenty-five years experience investing in hedge funds, either personally or institutionally, and each knew Mike for more than ten years. They testified as to Mike's expertise in what he did. They gave him high marks and high praise.

The defense attorneys did an excellent job of highlighting the testimony of Ms. Molberg and the three investors who testified for him. They also did an excellent job of discrediting the prosecution's witnesses. Mike had the feeling that he would soon be exonerated and would be returning to London with his family. But what the attorneys could neither control nor anticipate was the poisonous effect that Juror #7 would have on the jury pool. This juror, with an overbearing and bullying personality, was out to get Mike, and she would not be denied. She even posted on Facebook that she was on a jury and the defendant was a Wall Street type she referred to as "slimy", or some such wording to that effect. Her mind was made up before the testimony and evidence were even presented. Throughout the jury deliberations she let her opinion be well known.

After a two-week trial the prosecution and defense rested. The date was December 18, 2013, just a few days before the holiday break. The judge was in a hurry to finish up. The jury, with Juror #7 calling the shots, was in a bigger hurry. The judge spent three hours reading the charges to the court. It was a complicated case, and he understood that it might be difficult for the jury to grasp all the technical nuances. But in an outrageous miscarriage of justice, the jury spent only about an hour deliberating. Even the prosecution was amazed at the speed at which the verdict was returned. Juror #7 got her way. Mike was pronounced guilty of securities fraud, conspiracy to commit securities fraud, and wire fraud.

The following day Mike's attorney received a call from Juror #9. In that call the juror said that he had been bullied by Juror #7 into voting to convict, that his conscience bothered him about that, and that when he told his wife what had happened she insisted that he call the attorney to confess. He also said that he had been speaking with Juror #11 who had said the same thing. These jurors' failure to live up to their obligation, and their personal cowardice in the face of withering harassment by Bully #7, led to a verdict they had never intended.

The months following Mike's conviction were spent in trying to limit the damage to Mike's life. The probation department did its investigation with a view toward establishing the damage that Mike's actions had caused (using the assumption that because of the guilty verdict, there must have been damages.) In its Pre-Sentencing Report (PSR) probation basically went along with whatever information the prosecution fed it. At first the prosecution said there were 280 victims. That number was later revised to nineteen. And it said there was a loss to victims of $390 million. It also said that more points should be assessed because there was an international conspiracy, and that Mike was guilty of abuse of power because of the influence he had with respect to the Millennium fund. On the sentencing table probation arrived at a number of points that was nearly off its own scale. With that many points, and the amount of money involved, much like the case of the notorious Bernie Madoff, a sentence of life in prison would not have been out of the question.

In a pre-sentencing brief Attorney Tacopina argued that there was no loss on account of the activities for which Mike had been convicted. That the Millennium Fund had lost a lot of money for its investors was true, but that was not why Mike was convicted. He was convicted on the charge that he had overvalued one of the assets in the fund he was managing. In the real world, the logical world, beginning with Probation's early calculation of points, this equates to an unlimited term of incarceration. Subtract out the $390 million loss, (and if there was no loss, there can be no victim), and the resultant points would be perhaps one third as many as had initially been calculated. That would call for zero to eighteen months in prison, but more likely a period of supervision as oppose to incarceration, and no restitution. On the matter of the dollar loss to investors, Attorney Tacopina requested a Fatico Hearing, which all defendants are entitled to when money losses are at issue. In a Fatico Hearing an independent panel is convened to study the facts and arrive at a dollar figure for the loss. The judge denied the attorney's request for that hearing.

During the six-month period between his conviction and sentencing, not only were the prosecution, probation, and defense attorneys busy filing reports and briefs, but also other forces were at work to try to help Mike along. The judge received seventy-three letters from friends, family members, colleagues, and investors attesting to Mike's good character. These letters were heartfelt sentiments attempting to influence the judge into seeing a different kind of person than the prosecution was trying to portray. The expression of support for Mike was profound and had its intended effect on the judge in his final determination.

The day of sentencing was June 23, 2014. It was a roller coaster day of high anxiety for Mike. In a four-hour hearing, Attorney Tacopina pointed out that the sentence should be mitigated by the fact that the government had not produced a single victim; nor had it received a single complaint from any of Millennium's investors. That was good, and Mike felt hopeful. But when the judge said he was going to use the government figures with respect to the amount of the loss and the number of victims, Mike knew that was bad news. His uncomprehending head told him he might be sent away for twenty years, fifty years, or life. He began to tremble and broke out in tears. Nothing in his life had ever affected him so profoundly. He thought his life was over, and the thought of suicide entered his head. But when the judge suggested that he would impose non-guideline sentence, and the prosecution did not object, Mike saw a ray of hope. Anything had to be better than the gruesome result he was dreading.

At the end of the marathon hearing the judge finally ruled. Mike was sentenced to four years in prison, followed by three years of supervised release, and ordered to pay $390 million in restitution. The prosecution wanted Mike to be immediately remanded (taken into custody). Tacopina objected, the judge sustained the objection and released Mike under his bond. Four months later, Mike self-surrendered to the Federal Prison Camp at Pensacola, Florida, to begin serving his sentence.

Many articles have been written regarding the Michael Balboa story. His name has appeared in Internet blogs, newspapers, and magazines all over the world. Supporters want to know why Preet Bharara reached across the Atlantic to try a fund manager who had broken no laws in his own country, or for that matter, in America. How many millions of dollars did the prosecutor spend in investigating the case and flying witnesses into New York, and paying their expenses for weeks at a time after the defendant had been cleared of wrongdoing by so many other agencies? The prosecutor made a big splash. At Mike's expense he bolstered his own reputation. But at the end of the day, after ruining this man's life, and doing inestimable damage to the Balboa family, did he ever get that promotion to Washington that he was posturing for? No, he did not! In fact, when Donald Trump took office in 2017, Bharara was one of the first federal prosecutors to be sacked.

A Prosecutor Blunders – Everybody Pays
The Story of Dr. Joe Piazza

When prosecutors become overzealous in their pursuit of indictments, this behavior frequently results in epic miscarriages of justice. The case of Dr. Joe Piazza of Ft. Lauderdale, FL, is an example of just such an instance.

For all his life Joe knew he wanted to be a doctor. He also knew what the price to attain that goal would be in terms of schooling, residency and internship. Born and raised in Brooklyn, NY, Joe came from a hard working middle class family. His father was a commercial photographer of such things as print advertisements and weddings. His mother was a seamstress. Knowing that he would need a top-notch education to achieve his goal of becoming a doctor, Joe did restaurant work after school, weekends and summers to pay his way through Brooklyn Prep. This was a private high school with a reputation for its rigorous academic curriculum. He also worked his way through Boston University where he studied pre-med courses and graduated Magna Cum Laude in 1973.

Joe's decision to attend med school at Italy's University of Palermo had its benefits and drawbacks. On the downside he would have to repeat all the pre-med courses he had taken at BU; and he would have to become fluent in Italian. The entire process, including med school and residency would take ten years followed by a two-year fellowship for his cardiology specialty. On the plus side, his tuition at Palermo was free, meaning he would not be saddled with hundreds of thousands of dollars in student loans when he completed schooling, and it was there that he met his lovely wife Ada.

In 1980 Joe returned to the U.S. After passing his ECFMG (Educational Commission for Foreign Medical Graduates) he did residency work at Down State Medical Center in Brooklyn, and at Mt. Sinai Medical Center in Miami Beach. After completing this work Joe set up a sole practitioner medical office in Ft. Lauderdale. Soon he had acquired an outstanding reputation as a bright and capable cardiologist specializing in non-invasive cardiovascular diseases. He was admitted to staff positions as six area hospitals where most of his work was performed in the intensive care units. For thirty-four years, between his cardiology practice and later his interpretation of vascular images, Joe was instrumental in treating on average 2,500 new patients a year. Of the 85,000 or so patients he helped, tens of thousands of lives were saved.

Year of diligent attention to his practice took its toll on Joe. By the time he was forty years old he suffered from hypertension, was thirty pounds overweight, and had three badly blocked coronary arteries. Having run himself into the ground, Joe decided to become his own patient. A full health work-up, followed by angioplasty, convinced him that if he wanted to live, he would have to make some lifestyle changes. Fortunately, with his medical background, he knew the formula for good health and a long life: eat right and exercise. Immediately upon his release from the hospital Joe began his new healthy routine, and within a year had gotten into tip-top condition. By the second year he had become a model for healthy lifestyles for middle-aged men.

During this period of rehabilitation and self-improvement Joe realized that a big part of his problem was centered around the demands of his job. Constant worrying about the condition of his patients, and calls in the middle of the night requiring him to rush to the hospital, took their toll. Joe wanted to be fit and healthy, not stressed and exhausted. In 2001 he closed his practice and took a job at Healthfair U.S.A., a medical imaging company. This company needed a doctor with Joe's credentials to read and interpret ultrasound images. The work was perfectly suited to Joe's qualifications. From home, or anywhere else there was an Internet connection, Joe could log on to the company web site and view the cases that were queued up for him. His computer monitor was the same technology he would have used had he been in the same office where the images were generated. In minutes Joe could perform a professional interpretation of a cardiac image and report the results to the company. He could easily perform 150-200 interpretations a day. He could then log off and his workday was over. He had no patients to worry about, no staff to process appointments and insurance claims, and no late night emergency calls to the hospital. It was a perfect situation. In fact, the job gave Joe so much flexibility that he purchased a home in Palermo where his wife still had a large family, and where there was reliable cable service for his image interpretation work. He split his time between there and his oceanfront condo in Ft. Lauderdale. Joe was now healthy and stress free and living the life he had earned for himself through years of hard work and study.

By 2009 Healthfair U.S.A. was having financial trouble. It was near bankruptcy and was forced to cut back on Joe's assignments. Believing the company would soon have to go out of business, he decided to seek alternative employment. He interviewed with Medical Express, the owner of Margate Pain Management in the town of Margate, Florida, a suburb of Ft. Lauderdale. Medical Express was owned by businessman Pasquale "Pat" Gervasio. Joe was impressed with the clinic. It appeared well run, it was in a professional medical center, and it had well-equipped examining rooms and a full nursing staff. One of the things Joe liked about the job was that he was able to establish his own quality control procedures for screening patients. He knew of the reputation and schemes of many pain clinics that were nothing more than "pill mills," and he wanted no part of anything like that. He was given free reign to set standards and to make certain that the clinic was practicing good and important medicine, and not catering to drug dealers and addicts.

Because Joe's previous specialty had been in the field of cardiology, he needed to take continuing courses and attend seminars in pain management. He received board eligibility in this specialty and received a dispensing license. One of the satisfying aspects of the job that Joe particularly liked was the relief he could give suffering patients. And some of them suffered greatly with conditions such as lupus, terminal cancer, multiple sclerosis, herniated disks, and dozens of other sources of intractable, debilitating pain. Joe was an angel of mercy to those poor suffering individuals, and he was enjoying the work.

In this clinic procedures were established to make certain it was treating real medical problems. It saw about twenty patients a day, by appointment only. It did not accept walk-in clients. Each patient had to bring his medical records so Joe could assess his/her needs. Then the medical records were verified by contact with the patient's previous medical facility. And finally identity checks were performed on each patient to make certain the clinic was not being fooled by imposters.

But Joe's tenure in this job was short lived. Several events came together that forced him into the decision to leave this job. For one, a regulation came about requiring pain clinics to be owned by doctors. Joe was not interested in that. At the same time Healthcare U.S.A. was being resurrected and wanted him back. After only seven months at Medical Express Joe left to accept the job with his previous employer. However, a great deal of damage had been done to Joe by Pat Gervasio and others in the short time he was there.

Pat Gervasio teamed up with businessman Richard McMillan III to open other, less reputable clinics in the neighboring communities of Boca Raton and Delray Beach. What Joe did not know was that the office manager, under instructions from Gervasio, was referring patients that Joe rejected to Gervasio and McMillan's other clinics. An addict or drug dealer who could not get his prescription from Joe could just drive a few miles up the road to Boca Raton or Delray to get his supply. By the time Joe left Medical Express in July 2010, Gervasio and McMillan had half a dozen clinics operating up and down the east coast of Florida that had doctors on staff to examine patients and write and fill prescriptions.

Not known to Joe at the time of his employment at Medical Express, the DEA and FBI had their eyes on the company. In fact, there were scores of other pain clinics, many of which were pill mills that were being investigated. With top- notch quality control measures in place Joe felt there was no reason for concern. He had always cooperated with the Broward County Sheriff's office, and on several occasions reported patients who were doctor shopping, that is receiving multiple prescriptions for powerful, addictive drugs from different facilities. Margate Pain Management had been audited by the Department of Health in January 2010 and passed with flying colors. By July of the same year Joe had left the firm to rejoin Healthfair U.S.A. and resumed interpreting cardio images.

Knowing nothing of what was going on back at Medical Express, Joe was content performing his interpretations for Healthfair and splitting his time between his homes in Ft. Lauderdale and Palermo, Italy. His routine consisted of daily cardio exercise, a perfectly healthy diet, and an interpretation workload what was enough to keep him busy and well paid, but not so much as to cause him aggravation. He was living the life, healthy, financially comfortable, and happy.

On June 11, 2011, a year after Joe's departure from Margate Pain Management, the Florida Department of Law

Enforcement raided the storefront clinics of Pat Gervasio and Richard McMillan III in a sweep they called Operation Silver Spoon. Gervasio, McMillan, four doctors and several office managers were arrested. These facilities were bold-faced pill mills dispensing only oxycodone and Xanax. When asked his opinion of why Gervasio and McMillan thought they could get away with operating in this fashion, Joe says, "The FBI had these guys on tape bragging they were making $250,000 a day. They were making so much money they thought they were bullet proof."

On September 8, 2011 Joe and Ada were passing through Miami International Airport on their return from Palermo. They were detained for questioning in the Customs office. They were searched, locked in a cell, and questioned for six hours. When they asked the purpose of this detention, no answer was forthcoming. By the time they were released they still had no idea as to why they had been detained.

Unknown to Joe at the time of his employment with Medical Express, the owners and managers of the clinics were using Joe's license and forging his signature to order excess quantities of drugs to supply their walk-in clinics. Joe admitted his responsibility for the legitimate drugs ordered for his patients, and successfully demonstrated that the invoices for the excess pills were forgeries. The prosecutor stipulated to that fact in his investigation.

Five days following their detention at the airport the reception desk at the Piazza's condo called up to say there was a gentleman there with a delivery. Ada went down to receive it. Here she met detective Kevin Scott of the Coconut Creek Police Department on detail to the DEA, and was presented with a Target Letter for Joe from the U.S. Attorney's office. Federal prosecutor Lynn Rosenthal was investigating Joe with a view toward charging him with illegally dispensing controlled substances, conspiracy to dispense controlled substances, and money laundering. At the time of the raid on the Gervasio/McMillan clinics there was also a warrant issued for the medical records of the Margate office where Joe had worked the previous year. In the search of those records Joe's name came up, and because of his position at that clinic, he had become a target of the investigation. Joe's case was treated as a federal matter whereas the cases of the other employees of Medical Express remained with the state.

In attempting to set the record straight with U.S. prosecutors, Joe's attorneys, Todd Weicholtz and William Shepherd, argued that Joe's activities were limited to his employment at a legitimate clinic, and the orders that Joe had placed with the manufacturer of the pain medications were legitimate. The prosecutor agreed to this, but there remained one matter unresolved. During Joe's tenure with Medical Express a patient with a previous problem with the law had secretly agreed to videotape one of his sessions with Joe. The patient was taken into an exam room where Joe put him through a battery of questions related to his condition and his level of pain. He received all the information he needed to make a thorough analysis and determination for appropriate treatment. He did not physically touch the patient, nor did he require the patient to disrobe so he could do a physical exam. He didn't have to, Joe knew this patient and he knew what he needed. It was a simple matter that precipitated all of Joe's coming problems and would irreparably alter the course of his life. He had failed to follow a simple standard procedure and paid for it with everything he had worked for his entire life.

The prosecutor gave Joe a Proffer Letter that he had no choice but to accept. Under advice of his attorneys he agreed to sit for questioning. In attendance at that meeting in the downtown office of the Federal Prosecutor were A.U.S.A. Donald Chase (he had replaced Lynn Rosenthal), Joe and his attorneys, the representatives of the FBI, DEA, IRS, and the Health Department. It was a five-hour interrogation wherein every aspect of Joe's involvement with

Medical Express was discussed, and the defense team was given a glimpse of what might be in store for Joe. It boiled down to this: Joe was going to admit to certain things that were done and plead guilty to the three charges spelled out in the target letter. If he chose to fight the charges and go to trial, the prosecution was prepared to ask for a minimum mandatory sentence. A.U.S.A. Chase threatened that he would charge Joe with illegally purchasing so much pain product that, if convicted, the penalty would be 240 months in prison. Additionally, there have been too many instances where defendants have testified in their own defense and been charged with "obstruction" thus giving them what is referred to as a "bump". A bump is extra points against a defendant, which can have the effect of requiring a longer sentence under the guidelines. In Joe's case that could have meant life in prison. His only remaining option was to plead guilty, save the prosecutor the time and expense of a trial, and agree to a sixty-month sentence. He objected to the quantity of 150,000 illegal pills as it had already been stipulated that all Joe's orders were legitimate. But the prosecutor insisted that it was an all or nothing offer.

In 1992 John Gleeson led the prosecution team that put crime boss John Gotti in jail for life. Now a federal Judge and advocate for sentencing reform, Judge Gleeson laments the changes in the process that now require minimum mandatory sentences. He writes. "Prosecutors' insistence on mandatory minimum sentences for minor players in the drug trade has warped the criminal justice system and robbed judges of sentencing authority. An addict who is paid $300 to stand at the entrance of a pier and watch for police qualifies for kingpin treatment." The law leaves the decision to prosecutors. Judge William Young of the Federal Court in Boston in a recent ruling wrote, "Prosecutors run our federal justice system today. Judges play a subordinate role, necessary yes, but subordinate nonetheless. We had a sentencing proceeding that involved no written submission, no oral advocacy, and no judging. It had all the solemnity of a drivers' license renewal and took a fraction of the time." Thus describes the system that Joe faced with these charges. He and his attorneys were powerless to fight back. The prosecutor had his own agenda and was armed with draconian consequences if Joe so much as raised his voice to defend himself.

In the end the sentence that Joe was given, and the charges that he had to admit to that he never actually did, were an abomination on the federal criminal justice system. In the plea he had to admit to having ordered five times as many pain and relaxation medications as he actually ordered. In spite of the prosecution's understanding about medications that Joe had ordered legitimately, Joe had to admit to those medications that were fraudulently ordered under his forged signature. The newspapers had a field day with Joe's admissions, painting him as a major purveyor of death. And since the newspapers and prosecution have the benefit of creating an argument with no rebuttal from the defense, Joe's humiliation was complete.

Joe had to make a choice between defending himself and facing a possible life sentence, or taking a plea that was being offered and spending sixty months in federal prison. Pat Gervasio and William McMillan III were out on bonds of $500,000 each awaiting trial in the state courts, and facing fifteen to twenty year prison sentences. Joe had no other choice but to take the plea. And since he pled guilty to a felony, the state pulled Joe's medical license. He will never again be able to practice medicine in the U.S. Not only was Joe's life ruined, but his family has suffered as well. Six months into his term in prison he learned that he would become a grandfather for the first time. So, not only will this injustice result in not being able to hold his first grandchild until it is perhaps three years old, but also the government has foreclosed on any possibly for Joe to go on helping critically ill and suffering patients.

A Pirate Looks at Thirty-Five Years
The Captain Ron Stansel Story

Captain Ron Stansel lived and worked on the water his whole life. The son of a sailor, Ray Stansel, Jr., who was the son of a sailor, Ray Stansel, Sr., Ron grew up on boats, commercial and charter fishing from Florida to Costa Rica, from Port Aransas, Texas, to Venezuela. Ron's father, Ray, Jr., was a versatile man having been trained in gyro systems during a stint in the United States Air Force, but also expert in sports fishing, commercial fishing, marine biology, and yacht handling. From their home in St. Petersburg, Florida, Ray, Jr. chartered out of the infamous smuggling center known as Hubbard's Pier.

In the late 1960s, during the summer months, the Stansels had a tradition of treating themselves to dinner out any day they caught 1,000 pounds of fish. They frequently made that mark in three or four hours of fishing. Some days they would return to the dock with a ton and a half of grouper and snapper. But there was bigger money to be made by men with the skills of Ray Stansel, and in later years his son Ron. They knew the Caribbean and Gulf of Mexico like their own back yard. They knew boat operations and navigation as well as anyone in the business. So, instead of earning $500 or even $5,000 a day commercial fishing, Ray, Jr. opted to earn up to $65,000 a day ferrying marijuana into western Florida's back bayous. A short time later he was turning thousands of dollars into millions of dollars, smuggling marijuana from South and Central America. Over time Ray became known as the Marijuana King, and one of the biggest marijuana smugglers in the world. It was no stretch to think that Captain Ron would follow in his footsteps.

Ron learned seamanship in the most practical way. From the time he was very young his father would place him at the helm and have him run the boat from offshore to the back bays and inland waterways of west central Florida. In 1972, when Ron was thirteen years old, he helped pilot the family's forty-foot Monroe from Tarpon Springs to Key West, with his father looking over his shoulder to ensure a safe trip. Over the course of several years Ray, Jr. built his fleet of eight commercial boats, and the family acquired a sizable net worth. But of course each load that was successfully carried north brought law enforcement that much closer to catching him. In June of 1973 the DEA made its move, and Ray Jr. was arrested and charged with conspiracy to import fourteen tons of marijuana. He was jailed at Morgan Street in Tampa, and his bond was set at one million dollars. This was one of the highest bonds ever imposed in the U.S. at that time. Several months, and several court hearings later, Ray, Jr. received a bond reduction to $500,000. His bond was promptly paid and he was free to go. On January 1, 1974 Ray, Jr. was reporting missing after failing to resurface from a dive he was making off Port Royal on the island of Roatan in Honduras.

From 1974, right after the disappearance of his father, Ron knocked around the waterfront in Tarpon Springs, cleaning boats, heading shrimp, doing odd jobs, and helping his mentor, T.P. Parrott to build a boat. In his mid-teens and fatherless, Ron had become somewhat rebellious. The 1970s and early 1980s saw large loads of marijuana being smuggled up and down the west coast of Florida and through South Florida. It was not unusual for a freighter loaded with 100,000 pounds of pot to tie up on the Miami River. It was also fairly common for shrimp boats, and other large commercial vessels, to arrive up and down both coasts of Florida from Colombia, carrying ten to thirty tons or more of pot. Hundreds of recreational boaters and sport fishermen were making big paydays. But Ron never liked working in Miami. With the influx of Marielitos, that is criminals having been released from Cuban prisons, and Cocaine Cowboys out of Colombia, the life of a drug dealer or smuggler was hazardous. During this time Ron became a smuggler, dealer, and broker working out of the west coast of Florida.

In 1979, Ron and two partners purchased a forty-foot Morgan with the intention of commercial shrimping. But when the 597-foot long bulk carrier Summit Venture ran into the Tampa Skyway Bridge resulting in the collapse of a portion of the bridge and the loss of twenty-six lives, the Morgan was converted for use as a salvage boat. It ferried engineers and scuba divers to the site of the wreckage seven days a week. The three owners took turns operating the boat.

During this same period, on a skiing trip to Colorado, Ron was introduced to some people who were interested in doing business with him. Ron worked it out that on his two out of three days off the boat, he would smuggle small quantities of cocaine, usually less than a kilo, between southern Florida and Boulder, Colorado, an affluent community that is the hometown of the University of Colorado. Eventually that business grew into a much bigger operation where he would arrange for loads of marijuana coming out of Belize, Colombia, Panama, and Jamaica to be transported to one of the biggest distribution centers in the country, Ann Arbor, Michigan.

All the while Ron was smuggling, selling, and brokering marijuana, he kept a legitimate job either servicing the salvage operation, or shrimping, or commercial fishing. For a while he was a land surveyor, and at other times he delivered yachts all over the Caribbean and Gulf of Mexico. He had a policy that said that anyone who worked for him either as a mate, or as a driver, or an unloader, had to have legitimate employment. Men just sitting around getting high and waiting for the next load are a target for law enforcement. All of Ron's employees and agents had to look and stay busy.

Even before 1990, the Drug Enforcement Agency was wise to what was happening throughout Florida and the Caribbean. Loads were being seized and people were going to jail. Ron had a sixth sense about cops and managed to avoid the law. But seeing friends and acquaintances being arrested made him uneasy. He was losing sleep and becoming paranoid. At one time his wife, Angela, thinking that it was just too coincidental that Ron had not been arrested, asked if he was cooperating with the law. Ron flew into a rage. He would never do such a thing. But that conversation hit home with him. There was just too much heat, and Ron had been pushing his luck. Fortunately he had developed a lifestyle that allowed him to keep moving all the time. He was a constant traveler, and he knew a lot of nice places where he could live happily out of the reach of the DEA.

For most of 1988 and 1989 Ron and Angela sailed around the Caribbean. Their port of call was St. Thomas in the U.S. Virgin Islands. But, after two years as vagabonds, they decided on another more traditional lifestyle in Florida. They found a nice place in Pass-A-Grill on the west coast and moved in. Upon returning to Florida, Ron continued dealing in large quantities of marijuana. The stress of the situation contributed to a rift in the family, and Angela separated and returned to live in St. Thomas. Rather than living alone in the house, Ron moved back onto the family sailboat.

Drug busts were becoming a constant occurrence, and dealers were lining up to testify against others to get the best deals possible from the FBI and DEA. Ron would have no part of that. At one point he found a tracking device on his boat, so he knew he had become a target. He completely exited the business for a while and got a job selling marine electronics.

Because of the effectiveness of the DEA and FBI in shutting down drug smuggling in Florida, Ron discovered that there was a void in the delivery mechanism for drugs being smuggled out of Colombia. He decided that he would make one more run: have a big payday, and quit the business permanently. Through a friend Ron learned that there was a 600-kilo load that needed to be picked up off the coast of Jacksonville, Florida, and brought ashore. Ron offered to rendezvous with the freighter and carry the load as far as the sea buoy. He demanded a million dollars, because the risk of being caught carried a life sentence. The sponsors of that load balked at his price and said they had someone who would do the deal for a quarter of that amount. Ron encouraged them to take the other offer and walked away. Six weeks later the same agent came to Ron with another proposition from the same source. He could make a seven-figure payday by meeting a 500-kilo load of cocaine off the coast of Rio Hacha, Colombia, and bringing it back to offshore Tampa. With his brother, Ray III, and a greenhorn mate, they set sail for the San Blas Islands on what was calculated to be a twenty-six day trip. But in a sailing situation, where the best a sailor can hope for is to move forward at about six to eight knots, and where weather more than a week out is uncertain, anything can go wrong. On this trip that is exactly what happened. On the way down the boat was boarded by the U.S. Coast Guard off the coast of Cuba. They found nothing out of the ordinary, but it appeared as a bad omen. Shortly after the boarding, the boat began to develop electrical problems. Ultimately it was determined that the best course of action was to return to the Florida Keys where they could get dependable repairs. He was now running far behind schedule, but every time Ron contacted the broker he was told the deal was still on.

After countless hours of exhausting troubleshooting, the electrical problems were solved. Ron and crew set sail from Key West for the coast of Colombia. Several days into the trip they ran into a storm the likes of which Ron had never seen. Waves as tall as the top of the mast pounded them from every direction. The boat was knocked down, meaning it was pushed over on its side, nearly upside down. The cabin contents were tossed around and the electronics were destroyed. Anything lying on the decks was washed overboard (except for Ron who had wisely tied himself to the railing of the cockpit). The mainsail was blown out, and the propeller was fouled in one of the sheets, leaving the boat helpless with the exception of a small Genoa sail. The crew limped along under sail until the waves subsided and Ron could swim under the boat to cut out the fouled line. This made it possible for them to motor into Colon, in Panama, to begin repairs to the boat.

After repairs the crew returned to the sea to complete the arrangements. While in transit the location for the pickup was changed. Ron was told to meet the load in Isla de la Muerta, thirty miles off the Colombian coast. Having no charts of the area (the change was unexpected and he was not prepared for it) Ron luckily came across a sailor who had just left the area and could help him out. From the sailor's charts Ron copied the important information he would need to wend his way to the rendezvous point through shallow waters and coral heads. Ron and his crew spent ten days waiting to be contacted for the pickup. Tensions were high and Ron had a great deal of trouble controlling his crew's emotions. Finally the load made its way to where Ron was waiting for it, and he was able to take off for the delivery point offshore of Tampa. On the way home Ron carefully hugged the coasts of Costa Rica, Nicaragua, Belize, and Mexico on the track north. He crossed over to offshore Tampa where the load was picked up by a small offshore fishing boat. In the end, the venture was successful although they were presented with several life-threatening situations. It took three months to accomplish what had been scheduled for less than a third of that time.

The expedition to Colombia left Ron a well-to-do man, not mega bucks, but comfortable for years to come. He decided to return to St. Thomas to visit his daughter, Hannah, and explore the possibility of reconciliation with Angela. While visiting the island Ron received a call from his long time friend, partner, and attorney, David Young. In a somewhat cryptic message he was told not to come back to Florida, that there were weird things going on, and there was heat. He was told to head south. Ron and Young made plans to meet up in Costa Rica. Several days later, in a subsequent call, Ron was asked why he was still in the Virgin Islands. Young reiterated the urgency of the situation inasmuch as being in the U.S. Virgin Islands was the same as being anywhere else in the U.S. His arrest and incarceration there would create no extradition hurdles. In other words - get the hell out of there now! Ron booked passage on the first plane out of St. Thomas, a flight headed to Caracas, Venezuela. From there he proceeded to Colombia to see some business associates, and then on to Panama on his way to Costa Rica.

In San Jose, Costa Rica, through some fortuitous events, Ron made friends with a group of wealthy Americans who were set up with vacation homes in the area of Flamingo. A beautiful oceanfront apartment became available to him and he jumped at the opportunity to rent it. Ron had landed in paradise where he would begin a new life in a style that most people could only dream of.

David Young flew into San Jose to meet up with Ron, to bring him some money to live on, and discuss the troubles back home. Months before, in a conversation with Young, Ron had asked questions related to the way he had always operated. For example, when Ron was smuggling large quantities of marijuana and cocaine throughout the Caribbean he always kept the load on deck with heavy lead weights so that if a Coast Guard or DEA boat approached he could jettison the load in less than one minute. David told him that unless they caught him with the drugs there was little they could do. It seemed that anything Ron asked resulted in an answer that would have kept him safe. But

Ron did not ask the right question. Had he asked about the consequences of others giving testimony against him, he might have gotten a lesson in conspiracy laws that would later become his undoing.

Ron was fully convinced that his best course of action was to move out of the states permanently, and this suited him well. He had a beautiful life complete with oceanfront living and a gorgeous, adoring Chilean girlfriend. Meanwhile, back in Florida, a wannabe drug kingpin by the name of Desmond Valdez had been busted on drug charges and turned informant for the government. Valdez was also a client of David Young. Valdez did not know Ron personally, but he did know Sam Sliger and John Sholer, who had been friends and associates of Ron's in the business. By this time Valdez was singing like a bird, and bringing down anybody he could find in an effort to improve his position with the authorities. By cooperating Valdez could be released on bond. All this time his attorney, David Young, had no idea that Valdez was an informant.

On one particular occasion Valdez wore a wire for the feds and met up with Sholer to try and get more information. Sholer was high on mushrooms at the time and was being careless with his tongue. Valdez opened a conversation about having kilos of cocaine fronted to them. Sholer told Valdez that he would have to get them from Sam Sliger, but he couldn't get the quantities he wanted, as Sliger wasn't the owner of the product they had been selling. Sholer explained that Sliger worked for Stansel. When Valdez heard the name Stansel, he replied, "I know Ray Stansel." John told Valdez that it wasn't Ray Stansel, it was his brother, Ron, and that he lived down in Costa Rica, and controlled everything from there. That was the first time that Ron's name had ever come up in the entire investigation. When asked how Ron fit into the deal, Sholer told Valdez that Ron and Dave Young were best friends who grew up together.

The next time Valdez had a client conference with Dave Young he was wearing a wire. He led the conversation in such a way as to try to trap Young into saying something incriminating. The conversation turned to an associate by the name of Frank McLaughlin. Valdez voiced concern about McLaughlin being a problem, a "loose cannon." Unwisely Young uttered something to the effect that McLaughlin "needed to be eliminated." The feds had him. Conspiracy to commit murder at the very least. A big-time problem for the attorney. On his next trip the government knew that Young was going to Costa Rica to meet up with Ron. They stopped him at the airport before he left. They noted that he was carrying too much cash that he had not declared. Dave told them that the money was for gambling and prostitutes. He was actually bringing fresh money to Ron for living expenses, but the feds let him go. Young was clearly on the government's radar.

Shortly thereafter Ron received a call in the middle of the night from a friend in Tampa who knew what was happening. He was told that the police had taken Young into custody and that it would be only a matter of a few days before they figured out where he was located. He had to clear out immediately. Ron packed up what he could carry in a couple of suitcases and immediately split. He caught a bus out of Flamingo headed for San Jose. From there he caught a ride to the east coast of Costa Rica. He moved from an ultra modern apartment overlooking the Pacific Ocean to a $115 per month shack in the jungle on the edge of the Caribbean. He was the only gringo living on what the locals referred to as Rasta Row. It was located about six kilometers south of Puerto Viejo, a town of only a few hundred inhabitants. It was a pleasant place to live, but not what he was used to.

When Dave Young was arrested, Ron was cut off from his money. At a certain point, months after he had first arrived in Puerto Viejo, he was the poorest he had ever been in his life. He remembers a time when he had only thirty-five cents in his pocket. To get by he worked with a machete in the fields alongside peasant laborers. At times he was hungry. From being a well-to-do man, he had fallen back to third world poverty. His solace was that he was still free.

With a friend named Alan Bollinger, Ron helped to build a hilltop house overlooking the Caribbean. This gave him a nice place to live while he tried to get back on his feet. With a $20 gift from a friend, Ron opened a beachfront watering hole he called "The Spot". This was literally a piece of driftwood that he found on the beach to serve as his bar. He could make an icy drink of fruit juice and rum in a coconut shell. The drink was called Coco Loco. He was earning fifty cents to a dollar at a time selling drinks to tourists. From that he diversified into diving for spiny lobster, spear fishing, and hunting iguana. He became a source of food and drinks, and had started earning to get back on his feet. He turned the mountaintop home into a bed and breakfast, and lived a comfortable life in this paradise by the sea.

Ron had moved to Puerto Viejo in August of 1991. His indictment came down in December of that year. He had remained a free man in a most agreeable lifestyle for a year and a half, but all that was about to end. This was a time of what was called the Iran Contra Affair. Central America was crawling with U.S. Federal Agents. The U.S. Embassy in San Jose was a huge operation housing FBI, CIA, IRS, and DEA. The Ojeota, the Costa Rican secret police, move about among the citizens in civilian clothes, fitting in with the crowd. With an extradition treaty in place between Costa Rica and the U.S., the Ojeota cooperated fully with the U.S. agencies.

One day while Ron was enjoying a rum and coke with friends, sitting on the porch of a local bar, three Toyota Land Cruisers happened by. Ron didn't pay much attention, thinking it was probably a tourist group headed to a nearby resort. Even when the three vehicles came by in the opposite direction Ron took little notice. But when they returned again, and one of the Ojeota agents descended and approached him, Ron's cop radar went off. The moment that Ron had thought about for years, and dreaded more than anything, had arrived. But Ron would not give up without a fight. He punched the officer in the nose and knocked the other two undercover policemen down before he took off running. He knew that if he could make it 200 yards into the dense jungle he could escape. But as he ran to the jungle path his way was blocked by an agent twice his size. Not ready to give up yet, Ron kicked the giant squarely between the legs. The kick did bring the man down, but unfortunately he fell directly on top of Ron. Ron was pinned by the great man's weight, and seconds later was apprehended and placed in handcuffs.

Wearing only shorts and a t-shirt, Ron was taken to the town of Limon where he was placed in a cell. An agent of the U.S. Drug Enforcement Agency was present. The agent called the U.S. Attorney in Tampa to let him know that Ron was in custody. The DEA wanted to fly Ron back to Tampa immediately. At that time a certain individual back in Tampa by the name of Elliott Buckman had been indicted on drug conspiracy charges, and the DEA was prepared to make a deal on the spot if Ron would agree to give testimony against him. While others were willing to do so, Ron would have no part of it. As it turned out, in documents Ron later acquired through the Freedom of Information Act (FOIA), had Ron agreed to testify for the government, he would have been the only witness who not only possessed enough key information to destroy Buckman's defense, but he would have been the only reliable witness the government could produce. However, Ron adamantly refused to cooperate with federal authorities and Buckman was ultimately acquitted. Ron's refusal to cooperate with AUSA James Preston in the Buckman matter would later come back to haunt him.

The following day, still in shorts and t-shirt, Ron appeared before a Costa Rican magistrate. While the DEA tried to make a case for Ron's return to the U.S., the magistrate judiciously applied Costa Rican law. He asked Ron if he wanted to return to the U.S. Ron answered with an emphatic - No! Much to the disappointment of the U.S. authorities, Ron was taken to the San Sebastian prison near the capitol of San Jose. There Costa Rican authorities would not permit Ron's removal. Ron was being held in what is referred to as a diplomatic note. This process is in place when the U.S. State Department notifies the cooperating country that there is an outstanding indictment. When an extradition treaty is in place the cooperating country will place a diplomatic hold on that individual. It does not mean that the individual is under arrest in the foreign country, only that he is being held while the U.S. completes the process.

While Ron remained in San Sebastian fighting extradition, in an unrelated case of a fugitive from Wisconsin, that individual petitioned the Supreme Court of Costa Rica, the Sala Corte, to declare the extradition treaty between the United States and Costa Rica to be unconstitutional. In that action the court agreed and annulled the agreement. That move by the Sala Corte made front-page headlines in the Costa Rican newspapers, and Ron's name was mentioned as being affected by that decision. Ron's attorneys petitioned for his release based upon the fact that there was no agreement between the two countries by which he could be held or turned over to U.S. authorities. But the process was not that simple. The U.S. fought the petition and Ron remained in the Costa Rican jail until the issue could be cleared through the courts.

One day in July of 1993 several agents of Costa Rican immigration came for Ron. They placed him in handcuffs and moved him from San Sebastian to their immigration office near the San Jose airport. Ron was supposed to meet his attorney there to block his extradition from the country, as he had a petition for his release pending before the Sala

138

Corte. However, immediately upon his arrival at immigration headquarters, Costa Rican officials ran out to the parking lot to inform the immigration agents that they were transporting Ron. They said that the plane would be on the ground in ten minutes, and they had to get him to the airport. Upon his arrival at the airport, Ron was placed in a room where two U.S. Marshalls met him. They asked if he was ready to return to the states. Ron indicated that they could not take him, that there was no treaty between the United States and Costa Rica that would permit it. He repeatedly explained that he had appeals pending before the Sala Corte, and that to take him would be an act of kidnapping. Unmoved by his argument, the Marshalls placed Ron on a plane and escorted him back to Tampa.

In the middle of the night of July 13, 1993 Ron was booked into the Pinellas County jail. He was ushered into a room where his court appointed attorney and James Preston met him. It was not immediately explained to him that Preston was the Assistant U.S. Attorney in charge of the government case against him. In fact Ron did not know who the man was, or why he was there. He was given paperwork to read and sign. Those papers were a government form 5 K 1, Agreement to Cooperate. Ron became incensed, and ranted that he would never sign such an agreement, that he was innocent, and the government would never be able to prove a case against him. It was quite a display of temper in front of the enemy. From there he was transferred to the CCA (private/federal) correctional institute in Brookville, FL.

Ron had been given a court appointed attorney. In such cases the attorney's fee was far from adequate to defend him properly. The attorney told him that his case was winnable but that it would take at least 500 hours of preparation. The maximum attorney's fee government would pay was $3,600, not nearly enough for proper representation in a case this big. Ron called some friends who were able to put up money to hire a team of private lawyers, Jeff

Albinsom and Amy Williams, to represent him. Over the months that followed he and his attorneys worked on building his defense. The government had produced hundreds of hours of taped conversations and reams of documentation in the case against him. Ron was making a career out of compiling counter-arguments to everything the government had produced. What the government had was information based on hearsay and conjecture from unreliable sources. All of them had been proven to be liars in the past, and all of them had been given motivation to testify against him.

At a certain point while Ron was at Brookville, the Bureau of Prisons moved a jailhouse lawyer, an inmate named Donald Bean, into Ron's room to be his cellmate. Over the ensuing weeks Ron observed Bean helping many of the other inmates with their legal issues. Bean's apparent knowledge of the law convinced Ron that he could possibly help him sort through the thousands of pages of legal documentation to prepare for his trial. He decided to approach him about his case. Over the next several months Bean and Ron would spend many hours reviewing his case and preparing notes for his attorneys to use at trial. Bean had unfettered access to hundreds of hours of transcribed recordings of informants who were scheduled to testify against him. Much of the witnesses' testimony, as well as that of the government agents, was lies that Ron had the ability to refute. Bean was able to inform law enforcement officials that they had some serious issues to overcome if they were to counter-argue Ron's well researched position. But at this point the government had infiltrated the defense's camp. It knew all the questions that Ron and Bean had prepared for the defense attorneys. Earlier Ron had been warned by other inmates that Bean was a rat, but unfortunately he did not believe it. After spending months working together on the case, Bean and his contacts in the Customs Office had full knowledge of the facts at hand, and the strategy the defense would use. At a time when Ron was called to a hearing in Tampa, Bean was released. Ron later learned that he was a confidential informant, CI 103. With a trial date looming, and Ron no closer to entering a plea, the government had to try a new tack.

The time for Ron's trial was approaching. Ron's documentation was in order and his attorneys were prepared. On the Friday preceding the trial that was to begin on the following Monday, federal agents came to Ron's cell and removed all of his defense materials. Ron tried to protest that this was trial materials and privileged documentation. Without a word, the feds carted the documents away. On the following Sunday evening Ron's attorneys paid him a visit. They were in a somber mood; they had bad news. First of all, the prosecutor was going to bring new charges against Ron. He was going to be charged with conspiracy to import 600 kilos of cocaine. But worse, they were threatening to arrest his wife and several of his closest friends as co-conspirators. They said they would put Angela in a St. Thomas jail cell and, after a few months of that, she would surely break. The attorneys warned that if she gave testimony against him he was facing life in prison. Just a few days earlier Ron thought he would soon be winning his case and would be going home. Now he was facing a nightmare of epic proportions. The new deal was that the feds would drop charges against all the others if he would admit to conspiracy to smuggle five or more kilos of cocaine - in a case the government probably could not win. They had Ron in a corner, and he had no option but to give in.

The prosecution broke the law when it used information provided by Donald Bean to other law enforcement officials. That is a clear case of prosecutorial misconduct. Bean had set himself up as an aid to Ron in organizing his defense. As such he was privy to confidential, privileged information related to the facts of the case, and the strategy for the defense. He had reviewed thousands of documents and hours of tapes, and then fed this information about how the defense intended to use it to the investigators. This behavior is clearly prosecutorial misconduct, which if the law is to be justly administered, could result in sanctions, disbarment, or even prison. It was clearly an extreme abuse of power on the part of AUSA Preston, not only allowing this behavior to stand, but to allow it to continue for many months knowing that Ron was going to trial.

Once Ron was resigned to the fact that he was going to have to plead guilty to drug charges and spend time in federal prison, the next order of business was to posture for the best possible deal. There were a lot of issues to be considered. On the plus side, the prosecutor agreed to leave Angela and any of Ron's other friends out of the discussion. They would not be charged. But there was a lot more weight on the negative side. There was a large quantity of cocaine at issue, and there were other considerations complicating the deal. Years earlier Ron had served a period of probation on a marijuana bust. It was a small matter, but it left Ron with a prior conviction on his record. He was not a first time offender; he was now subject to an enhanced mandatory minimum sentencing of twenty years. He would have to serve 87% of this sentence before being eligible for release. By Ron's count he would plead guilty to transporting ten sail bags that contained approximately 350 kilos of cocaine, an offense that carried a twenty-year sentence. A horrible thought, but at least he was able to protect his family and loved ones.

September 6, 1994 was Captain Ron's sentencing date. In the courthouse holding area he was surprised to run into Sam Sliger. Ron had thought that his deal with the government had been set, but seeing Sliger, he realized that the government was posturing for a stiffer sentence. He questioned Sliger as to what he was doing there, and his response was an apologetic, "They own me." Sliger was testifying against Ron in order to get a better deal for himself.

Foolishly Ron thought that, because he had a written agreement with the government, the charges and his penalty had been set. But A.U.S.A. James Preston knew otherwise. Until a plea agreement is agreed to by the court, there is no deal. One feature of the plea agreement was that there would be no upward enhancement for the fact that Ron had special skills, his captaincy. As Sliger began to testify he started by saying that Ron was the captain of the vessel transporting the drugs. Had Ron's attorneys been alert they would have stopped the hearing right there and declared a breech of plea. Once that declaration was in place the plea negotiation would be concluded and the trial would begin. The attorneys had missed a perfect opportunity to save Ron from a tragic fate. The prosecution would do anything to avoid a trial. They knew their witnesses were a pack of liars. They knew that Ron had a solid strategy for his defense. And they knew there would be hell to pay for planting Donald Bean in Ron's cell and compromising his defense. Opening that one issue alone would point to a dozen cases where CI 103 had been involved, and which could have had the effect of providing food for appeals in dozens of cases. But the attorneys were blindsided by the government's last minute strategy, and outsmarted by an ambitious, if unscrupulous prosecutor. The judge in this matter stated that he was extremely unhappy with the way the prosecutor handled plea negotiations, and that by tricking and bullying the defendant it could make it difficult in the future for people to decide to enter into plea agreements. Preston responded to the effect that there might be legal issues involved, but that was the government's position.

In the Pre Sentencing Report (PSR), the Probation Department stated that there were 553 kilos of cocaine at issue in this case. It said that based completely on hearsay, having never confiscated nor seen any of it. Ron had admitted to 350 kilos. One of the major numbers in cases such as this has to do with whether the quantity is more than, or less than 500 kilos. Less than 500 kilos is a level thirty-eight offense carrying a twenty-year sentence. That would have been in line with Ron's expectations. But the court adopted the PSR and charged Ron with conspiracy to transport 553 kilos, a level forty offense that carries a 360-month sentence. To make matters worse, Ron received a two level enhancement for obstruction of justice, bringing his total level to forty-two, with a corresponding sentence of 360 months to life in prison.

The judge began from a level forty which carried a base sentence of 360 months. To that he added sixty months for the obstruction enhancement. Ron was sentenced to 420 months – thirty-five years in federal prison, plus ten years supervised release. He is scheduled to be released in 2023 after having been kidnapped in Costa Rica by the U.S. Government, having the government infiltrate his defense and threaten his wife, and based upon no physical evidence in the case, just the testimony of some very sketchy and unreliable witnesses.

Disaster after the Disaster
The Chris Benson Story

(Some of the names mentioned in this story are fictitious. Chris Benson considered those characters a possible threat to others, and asked that their identities be masked.)

When facing accusers, whether they are victims, police, or prosecutors, the defendant and his attorney can usually figure out long before sentencing where the battle lies. Most times in criminal matters it is a prosecutor who leads the charge on behalf of the public. And when plea bargains are ironed out, most often the agreed upon resolution is executed by the judge. But when Chris Benson and his attorney came to terms with the prosecution on a resolution of Chris' case, it was the probation department in its interpretation of the matters at hand that created circumstances that turned out to be a tragic miscarriage of justice, having devastating consequences for Chris, his young family, and his growing business.

New Orleans is one of the few cities in the world that are built below sea level and rely on seawalls and levies to hold back the sea. To geologists, meteorologists, and urban planners it was no surprise that when category five Hurricane Katrina hit in August of 2005, the city and surrounding area saw its worse flooding in recorded history. The destruction was epic. Seeing an immediate need for volunteers, Chris' natural instinct to help others took over. For his whole life Chris was a "go-to guy" for family and neighbors when there was a need. Always keeping busy either with his family, his work, his church, or community service, Chris had developed his own internally charged culture of helping. His strong spiritual beliefs made him recognize that he had been given gifts, and it was his obligation to use them to help others. He lived his life, always thankful for his good health, intelligence, and strong family support system. So, when the big hurricane hit, Chris spent days and weeks helping those who were left in worse condition than he. He helped lay tarps on damaged roofs, he spent days removing fallen trees from neighbors' property, fixed countless generators, played round robin with his own supply of generators so his neighbors' food could be kept frozen, and brought food, gas, and water to people in need. He stayed busy helping for as long as he could keep awake.

As the water receded and the area dried out, FEMA, the Federal Emergency Management Agency, the government agency that oversees the National Flood Insurance Program, introduced a program for private homeowners to raise their homes above flood level and avoid this kind of destruction in the future. A billion dollars were allocated to this project and a few enterprising contractors entered the arena.

At this time Chris was a small contractor building homes and doing remodeling jobs. Along with his wife, Becky, as the office manager/ bookkeeper they owned a company called Nelpac Construction. Chris saw the potential this new program presented. He decided to learn how the work was done and to enter that industry. The learning curve was an easy one for Chris. He had graduated cum laude from Southeastern Louisiana University. He knew a great deal about home construction and had received his contractor's license at the age of twenty-four. He saw the opportunity in the new FEMA program and set about educating himself on the complicated process of elevating houses. He rebranded his company, changed its name to Louisiana Home Elevations (LHE), and acquired the equipment necessary for the work.

In the process of raising a house there were structural, mechanical, electrical, site work, and permitting issues to be dealt with. Weeks of preparation went into readying a structure for a lifting process that took no more than a day or two. Chris had a network of sixty-seven different sub-contractors he could call upon to keep his work flowing. But Chris regrets the day he became associated with one of these subs, a man named Alfredo Ramirez (fictitious name). In the early days of the business arrangement Alfredo had the crews, and was a reliable, independent sub-contractor. But, unknown to Chris, Alfredo was employing undocumented workers. As time went on, Chris began to rely on Alfredo and his crews to do most of the site preparation work.

Alfredo did not trust banks and had no account of his own. Each weekly check with which Chris paid him had to be carried to a branch of CPB Bank that was an hour away. And sometimes these checks were for as much as $40,000. Alfredo told Chris that carrying that much money for that distance made him nervous and asked if he would give him checks in smaller, safer amounts. In the spirit of cooperation Chris agreed. Whether he wrote a single check each week or several made little difference. He authorized the favor within his company and never gave it another thought. It was an insignificant matter for someone in his office to write a few more checks each week. Alfredo was an IRS 1099 sub-contractor whose tax filing responsibilities were his own, and this arrangement should have no impact on Chris' accounting or bookkeeping system. He could not have been more wrong.

Over the course of about a year, as LHE grew, the quality of Alfredo's work began to deteriorate. Chris started contracting with others for the work that Alfredo had been doing. Then one day in March of 2011 when Alfredo's courier was returning from CPB Bank with cash, he was stopped by a local sheriff for a traffic violation. Realizing that this man fit the profile of an undocumented alien, the sheriff did a search of his car and found the cash for Alfredo's payroll. The suspicious sheriff seized the courier, the car, and the money, and hauled them all back to the precinct house. While questioning the courier, it was discovered that he was in the country illegally, so the sheriff called in ICE (Immigration and Customs Enforcement) to see if it wanted to get involved. ICE sent over an agent to interview Alfredo and open up a new case file. In that initial interview Alfredo, in order to deflect any wrong doing on his part, lied when he emphatically said that the courier was Chris' employee. He agreed to cooperate with the investigation and become an informant in exchange for heads other than his own.

During the time this information was being researched, Chris had no idea there was an ongoing investigation being coordinated between ICE and the IRS, and that he was the target of that investigation. Then on August 29, 2011, thirty agents from those two agencies raided Chris' office, busting through his unlocked doors, hands on their weapons, wearing SWAT gear, and looking very much like they were taking down a nest of dangerous terrorists. They took pictures, interviewed employees, and carted away computers and a mountain of documents. Simultaneous with the raid on the office, Alfredo had arranged for his workers to meet him for their payroll. When they arrived, the group was surrounded by ICE agents and taken into custody. To save his own neck Alfredo handed over Chris and his own loyal workers who now faced possible deportation.

Following the raid on the office, Chris was profoundly upset and needed to go home to tell Becky what had happened. It was a drive of only a mile or so. When he arrived home he noticed a government SUV parked outside his house. Alert to the possibility of another raid, Chris rushed into the house and quickly explained to Becky what had happened, and what he thought may happen next. He packed up Becky, the nanny, and his six-month-old son and sent them to the home of his in-laws a few miles away. Shortly after Becky drove off with her precious cargo, several more government vehicles arrived to carry out a search. When Chris showed reluctance to allow investigators into his home without a warrant, he was advised (threatened) with the facts about how this would play out. He was told he could voluntarily permit the agents into his home where they would carefully go through his records, take what they wanted, and allow him to make copies of important paperwork. In the event he wanted to remain obstinate and exercise his right to bar admission to his domicile without proper due process, they would secure the house for twelve to twenty-four hours and return with a search warrant. They made it clear that if he chose that option their search would be more thorough and they would toss the entire house. Chris spent the rest of the day copying important documentation he would need to continue operating, and worrying about the future and what this meant to the security of his family and the continuation of his business.

This whole episode caused a near riot among Alfredo's workers. They had not been paid, and now they had been targeted. When Alfredo's workers asked for their pay, he told them to seek it from Chris, even though Chris had already paid Alfredo for his work to date. Chris' foremen began receiving telephone threats about the payroll, and suspicious characters began driving through Chris' neighborhood. The workers were hungry for their paychecks and didn't care where the money came from. Alfredo went into hiding. Some very tough looking illegals began showing up in Chris' life. Because of the threat he felt toward his family, he moved them to several new hidden locations over the course of the next few months. Chris' anxiety level was through the roof. Not only was his company in jeopardy, and he had no idea what the prosecutor might have on his mind about how he would pursue the criminal case, but now he had to use all the wisdom and energy he could muster to protect his wife and children from physical harm. In discussions with his attorney, Chris suggested it would be easier and safer to simply pay the workers so they would leave him alone. But he was told that under no circumstances was he to do that. If he paid them, the government might be able to argue that he was employing undocumented workers.

At the time of the raids on Chris' home and office, the government impounded his company bank account. That account contained $627,000, the majority of which came from the government as grants to homeowners under the FEMA program. It was to be used to pay sub-contractors, suppliers, workmen, office workers, and other obligations of the business. The company had twenty-five homes "in the air" at the time, meaning these homes were in some stage of being raised; they were not habitable and they were vulnerable to further destruction and the possibility of collapse. The owners of these homes were temporarily living in motels and with relatives and would not be pleased at the prospect of having the completion delayed. Chris tried to make the government understand that he needed at least some of the confiscated funds to advance the work so no further damage would be done. But when the government failed to cooperate, Chris borrowed money so he could secure the properties and continue the work.

Conversations commenced between Chris' attorney and the special prosecutor, who was actually an attorney for ICE on assignment to the U.S. Attorney's office. Chris was dumbfounded by this entire experience and was certain of his innocence. Naively he expected that as soon as ICE and the IRS completed their investigation, they would realize that Chris and his company had done nothing wrong. They would see that this was a simple case of illegal aliens that worked for another company, and they would draft an apology, and that would be the end of it. He urged his attorney to set a meeting with the prosecutor and the agents from ICE and IRS. What he was expecting was a cordial sit down with these men where he would explain his position and talk some truth to them. But the meeting turned out to be much more hostile than Chris expected. After explaining his position and believing he had made himself clear, in as friendly a tone as he could muster, he asked what the next course of action might be. He was expecting to hear them say that this meeting had cleared things up. But instead what he heard from the prosecutor was that in the following week he would be going to the grand jury to seek an indictment, and that criminal charges would be filed. Prior to the ending of the meeting Chris' attorney asked the prosecutor for a courtesy call prior to filing charges so that he and Chris could be prepared for what to expect. The prosecutor agreed that he would make that call. He did not keep that promise, and the following week Chris was formally charged with hiring illegals, harboring illegals, financial structuring, and money laundering.

Approximately six months following the indictment, the prosecution made its first plea offer. In return for an admission of guilt to any one of the charges, it was up to the defense to pick which one, (they actually said, "We don't care which charge you pick.") The prosecution would also require Chris to sign a forfeiture agreement that in essence gave ICE the money they had confiscated. But by agreeing to this Chris would   receive a recommendation of no jail time. Chris now had to make a choice. Plead guilty with a near certainty of remaining free, or go to trial and risk a prison sentence. To Chris, the confiscated money was not the   issue. Most of it belonged to the state and it would be up to the federal government and the state to iron that out. But Chris believed in his innocence, and made it clear that he wanted to fight these unjust and unfounded charges.

To add more pressure to Chris, seven ICE agents showed up at the home of Chris' mother-in-law with a warrant to confiscate Becky's private automobile. In the home at the time were Becky, her mother, her aunt, the

151

nanny, and Chris' one-year-old son. Becky immediately called Chris to tell him of this raid. He sped home to try to control the situation. He railed at the agents, telling them that they did not have to terrorize these women and his young son, and that had they simply asked for the keys to the car through his attorney in a civilized manner, he would have given them with no trauma. The young agent leading the raid, full of himself and his own importance at the wearing of a Department of Justice badge replied, "That's just not the way we do things." Although Chris was a peaceful, law-abiding man and a devout Christian, that agent never knew how close he came to having his teeth knocked out.

During the period while Chris worked with his attorneys to fashion his defense, he also worked with the State of Louisiana on a solution to the problem ICE had created by confiscating the deposits of his customers. Time after time ICE promised to return that money to its intended parties, but in the end it kept the money and never made an accounting of it to the state. To its credit the state re-granted funds to those homeowners so that the work on their homes could continue.

Two months following the rejection of the first plea offer, the prosecution turned up the heat. It came to Chris with a second offer, but this one carried a threat. The same deal with respect to the forfeiture and a recommendation for no prison time was offered. Chris was warned that if he rejected the offer, the prosecution would file a superseding indictment, which meant that additional charges, and more potentially onerous consequences, would be added. Chris rejected the plea offer.

In order to get a sense of what it might expect if they went to trial, the defense team staged a series of mock trials. They used ordinary citizens as jurors. After several such mock trials the defense team was gratified to see that their chances of winning were better than fifty-fifty. Encouraged by these results, the defense was more than ever convinced the case could be won, and the plea offer was rejected.

In May of 2012, more than a year after the grand jury handed down its indictment, the date for the trial was upon them. The defense was ready with its arguments and rebuttals. Chris was ready. He needed to stage the performance of his life. He was innocent and this was his chance to prove it. (There was never a presumption of innocence on the part of the prosecution or the judge. It was always a presumption of guilt.) Chris, who was a hands-on contractor, often visiting his job sites in blue jeans, t-shirts, and boots, went out and bought some new suits, shirts, and ties for his appearances in court. He was ready; his defense team was ready.

Five days prior to the scheduled beginning of the trial the prosecutor's superseding indictment was filed. With a rash of new charges and demands, Chris was now facing many millions of dollars in fines and restitution, and decades in federal prison. And now, at the last minute, the prosecutor asked the judge for additional time to prepare its case. Counsel for the defense strenuously objected, stating that it was the prosecution who brought these charges, and it was the prosecution that should have had its case in order even before the charges were filed. This was the prosecutor's show and they all wouldn't be there if it had conducted a legitimate investigation into the alleged matters. In a gross miscarriage of justice, the judge ruled in favor of the prosecution and set a new trial date for the end of the year.

The following six months was punctuated with pre-trial preparations. Another mock trial was staged, expert witnesses were interviewed, and extensive coaching of Chris as a defendant took place. Chris' second child was born during this time, thus compounding his responsibilities to his growing family. After months of preparation, hundreds of thousands of dollars spent to protect himself; after more sleepless nights wracked with worry, the eleventh hour was upon them. The trial would be in five days. They were ready and they were going to win.

But all that changed with a single phone call. Chris' lawyers called to tell him that they received another offer from the prosecutor, and this time it carried a more serious threat. If he doesn't take the offer, they will indict his wife in three days. This vulgar threat shook the entire Benson family to its core. The idea that Becky could be a target was unfathomable. Becky, high school class president, homecoming queen, and sweetheart of the town. Becky attended Southeastern Louisiana University on a full academic scholarship, and for years worked in law enforcement as a crime scene investigator and fingerprint expert, would be a target of this grotesque witch hunt. It was inconceivable that any prosecutor, no matter how ambitious or corrupt, could use such a tactic. But this was the threat, and it created a whole new paradigm for the defense.

When the prosecutor put forth this threat the dynamics of the case changed. Under no circumstance, regardless of Chris' degree of guilt or innocence, could this risk be taken. Defense counsel had impressed upon Chris the fact that the judge would recognize that this threat had forced Chris' hand, and he would consider this in his sentencing decision. Chris agreed to plead guilty to a single charge of financial structuring, specifically, instead of writing one check for $12,000, Chris wrote one for $9,000 and one for $3,000. The amount of the structuring was less than the $30,000 threshold that, for sentencing purposes would equate to zero to six months in prison. But based upon Chris' profile, lack of previous criminal history, and ties to the community, the judge would probably accept the plea and rule to accept the $627,000 forfeiture with no jail time.

Then came the time to sit for the pre-sentencing interview. Such interviews are conducted by the U.S. Probation office. The facts of the case as presented by the prosecution are analyzed in light of the statements by the defense about his own background. From that, probation generates a PSR (Pre-Sentencing Report), which is presented to the judge for purposes of determining a sentence. The Criminal History Calculation is a matrix that combines the category of crime with the severity of the offense to come up with a point system used to determine the amount of sentence a convicted person might receive. Chris' attorneys believed that his charge for Financial Structuring, that is, being involved in a scheme to use the banking system in such a way as to avoid reporting requirements, would be a minor matter. Cash transactions of more than $10,000 must be reported by the banks. Alfredo was cashing checks for less that this amount, but he was laying the fault on Chris. The prosecutor was happy to take sides with Alfredo. Chris' "guilty conduct", a term related to criminal cases, that is, the amount of checks either written by or signed by Chris amounted to $12,000. His guilty conduct was below the $30,000 threshold for sentencing. A calculation this low rarely results in a prison sentence. But Probation made its assessment based upon "relevant conduct", which took into account all of the business done between Alfredo and Chris' company. Relevant conduct in this instance amounted to $1.5 million, and raised Chris' points from the expected eight, to twenty-six. Now they were talking about some serious prison time. Probation recommended a five to six year prison term. The prosecution had no objection to probation's recommendations in spite of their agreement not to pursue a prison sentence. In response to the first draft of the PSR, defense counsel prepared a forty-eight page pre-sentencing memorandum. In that document defense objected to six basic issues upon which the point assessment had been calculated.

Chris was told by his attorneys that there was virtually no chance of jail. The pre-sentencing brief they filed would dispel all those extra points that probation had added up against him. Chris was told that the judge would see through the prosecution's strong arm tactics and rule in favor of the defense. He was confident that he would go to court and come home the same day. At sentencing the courtroom was packed with his supporters. More than one hundred people showed up, and scores of letters bearing witness to Chris' character were written. The judge commented that he was impressed with this level of interest, and that he had never seen such an outpouring of support.

Then came the time for the judge to rule on the pre-sentencing memorandum from the defense. As he went through the document, he very mechanically rejected the defense rebuttal item by item. Each item would have taken points away from the punishment schedule. It looked as if the judge was a bought-and-paid-for agent of the prosecution. The process could not have been more prejudicial to the defense. With each stroke of the pen Chris' heart sank deeper and deeper, as the judge took the liberty of cutting the defense to shreds. After completing his review of the brief, the judge took off on a discourse using terms such as "guilty of the charges" and "the pronouncement of sentence" and "you knew these acts were illegal". Meanwhile Chris' perception was changing with every word and every stroke of the judge's pen. From a positive outlook, confident that no jail time would be forthcoming, he now realized that his entire future was at stake. His points were a multiple of what his attorneys told him to expect, so he now had a sinking feeling, and came to the realization that this judge was going to put him away. The judge shifted in his chair from right to left, left to right, as he thought about how he would make Chris pay for the crime he did not commit. Chris' heart pounded in his chest as thoughts of his young family's future raced through his mind. It could be ten years; it could be twenty. No matter what, Chris' life as he once knew it was over. As if ordering toast to go with his eggs, or a pair of socks to go with his new shoes, with no more concern for Chris' future than he might have for what the weather might be next weekend, the judge finally made up his mind: twenty-one months in federal prison. Twenty-one months because the ICE prosecutor chose to pursue the case based upon the testimony of the real perpetrator of the crime. Twenty-one months because the prosecutor was able to force an admission of guilt under the threat of prosecution of another innocent party, Chris' wife. Twenty-one months and $627,000 of other people's money because it was a profitable result for ICE regardless of the fact that many innocent people were deeply affected by the results of the process. A family, a career, and a future destroyed because it was easier and more profitable to pursue the case the easy way, as opposed to looking for the truth and punishing the people who actually broke the law.

Throughout the investigation agents interviewed many of LHE's sub contractors. Later one of these subs came to Chris to tell him of his experience with the investigator. Referring to Chris, the agent told that individual, "You don't have to worry about anything. We just needed to make an example of someone, and this guy had substantial enough assets to make it worth our while."

Torture
The James Watkins Story

(All of the names in this story are fictitious as are the locations. James Watkins is a fictitious name. Concerned for the safety of himself, family, and friends, the subject character asked that no real names be used. The events described in this story are real.)

The wide net of conspiracy has often been used as an abusive tool of federal prosecutors. Misused it can be the source of great hardship to innocent people. Is every person who is a party to a transaction a co-conspirator when one person involved in the transaction breaks the law? This is the story of James Watkins, a successful real estate broker, who was caught in the snare of an ambitious prosecutor. He was indicted for a crime he had no part in committing. It is the story of abuse of power by a dishonest federal agent, a federal judge who refused to listen to, and in the end threatened the defendant, as he tried to explain why his role in the transactions at hand was in no way related to the crime. It is the story of a man who got caught up in the criminal justice system and was subjected to torture and deprivation at the hands of federal marshals. And it is the story of a sad set of circumstances that repeats itself too frequently in the criminal justice system.

At age twenty-three James Watkins was retired. He had been working since he was a young boy, but now he had enough saved that if he worked his money and invested judiciously, he would never have a boss. But in a short while James learned that retirement was not what he thought it would be. He was not built for the lifestyle of leisure and aimless inactivity that goes along with the common perception of retirement. All of his contemporaries were busy working, building careers, and doing deals. James's ambition and restlessness required that he too remain active in business.

He was born in Falls Church, Virginia, in 1945. Because his father had anger and alcohol issues, when James was eight years old he was placed in a foster home until Child Welfare could have him placed legally in a safe, permanent home. It was in this foster home that he met another foster child, Maureen Toll, whose parents had died, and who was awaiting placement. Maureen and James played together all the time. They were best friends. But they were separated when Maureen was adopted by a new family. James promised at that time that someday he would come looking for her and he would find her. Shortly thereafter James was sent to live with his aunt and uncle on a small farm near Lake George in upstate New York. The farmhouse was Spartan with no indoor running water, and the toilet was an outhouse. The place was mainly a dairy farm with about seventy-five cows, thirty goats, and 500 chickens. The farm sold cows' milk, goats' milk, cheese, chickens, and eggs. Before he was ten-years old James was doing the work of a grown man, helping to maintain the farm and feed the family. In a good year the family earned about $7,000. James attended public schools, and every Sunday he and his aunt attended services at the Catholic Church. Bible reading was a daily event.

When he was about sixteen years old James went looking for his old friend, his best friend, Maureen. He had not seen her in nearly a decade but he thought of her everyday. It was an exhausting search that lasted for two years. James received no cooperation from anyone who could help, but with grim determination he pursued his quest until he found her. Upon seeing each other again, they courted for several years and committed to each other.

In the early 1960s an event occurred that influenced James and set him on a path to success in real estate. A man James describes as looking like the Monopoly man, black suit, bald head, and handlebar mustache, showed up at the farm in a big shiny black Cadillac. The man was the picture of success. He had a buyer who was interested in the farm. An offer was made, the aunt and uncle liked the price, $500,000, and the transaction was consummated. The Monopoly man walked away from the closing with $50,000. When James saw this huge commission for so little effort, he decided that real estate was a career worth considering for himself.

When the farm was sold, James's aunt and uncle retired to Florida, so he moved back in with his parents. His father was very ill at the time, too weak to be a threat to anybody, and soon passed away. James left school, but took courses to complete his high school diploma, and graduated ahead of his class. At the same time he received his real estate license and purchased his first property. It was a run down two-story home, badly in need of rehabilitation. But the price, $1,000, was within the range he could afford. With a bank loan and a lot of sweat equity, James turned that property into a three-story house completely finished and in move-in condition. He had invested $8,000 in the property and sold it for $24,000. With that transaction complete he was able to buy two properties, rehab them, and continued to double and triple his money. Then he bought four houses, and before long he had bought, rehabbed, and sold over thirty properties, including several small apartment buildings. His goal had been to work until he was thirty and retire. The real estate business was exhausting. He owned a number of rental properties and tried to maintain them all himself. The endless calls from tenants at all hours of the day and night wore him out. By 1968 James had bought and sold several millions of dollars of real estate. He had a substantial net worth in cash and mortgages receivable. He was twenty-three years old and semi-retired.

At this time James and Maureen built a home near Green Bay, Wisconsin, and were married. But they were young, free, and adventurous, and had the cushion that would allow them to travel and enjoy themselves. For two years they toured North and South America and the Caribbean. For the last part of the journey they spent about a year traveling around the United States in an RV, visiting nearly all of the lower forty-eight. But this lifestyle soon became tiring and they decided to return to their home in Green Bay. James did occasional real estate brokerage deals, but wasn't serious about it. In 1979 he traveled to Florida on a business trip. He was impressed with the beauty of the place and the agreeable climate, having just left the freezing snow of Wisconsin for the sunny beaches of Florida. James loved the ambiance. He and Maureen discussed it, and soon they relocated to Ft. Meyers.

Florida real estate law requires that licensees hold a salesman's license for a period of two years before being eligible for a broker's license. So James signed up with a nationwide realty firm and received his salesman's license. He sold real estate part time while he developed a business model for specialized commercial real estate brokerage. He wanted to be a force in the hotel/motel brokerage business. He started at the tip of Florida in Key West. He visited every hotel and motel in his path, interviewing clerks, managers and owners, asking if they would be interested in selling their property or acquiring a new one. He knew he would meet with rejections 90% of the time, but it was the other 10% that was his focus. James worked his way up U.S. 1 and A1A, knocking on hotel and motel doors all the way from Key West to Jacksonville. He built a vast database of information with specifics about the properties and contact information on the owners. When he was done with that, he crossed the state and worked his way from Panama City to Fort Myers.

161

Once that was done he worked his way back up the middle of the state through the motel-rich Kissimmee, Orlando, and Disney areas. And throughout the state he was keeping busy matching buyers with sellers of these specific types of properties. By 1982, just two years into this project, he had become the largest broker of hotel/motel properties in the State of Florida. This was a great business James had created for himself; he was making a lot of money, sometimes as much as $200,000 on a single transaction. But money was never his only goal. Lifestyle was everything to him; that is, a manageable pace where he could work, and at the same time enjoy time with Maureen. James was an uncomplicated man, looking for a simpler life. In 1989 he and Maureen made the decision to quit that business and travel some more.

Feeling that his life was becoming too much work and not enough play, James folded his real estate tent, and he and Maureen headed to Hawaii. For three years they settled on the Big Island where they enjoyed the beaches and fishing in Kona. Not knowing exactly where they wanted to resettle, having gotten all Hawaii had to offer for them, they decided to begin moving toward Florida, but with an open mind to any possible places they might like to settle in along the way. They made it as far as Long Beach, California, and found an area they liked. They settled there for about a year and then moved on. Ultimately they landed in Florida again, but not before sampling Texas and Puerto Rico. This vagabond lifestyle was something Maureen cherished. She loved to travel and was curious about the world around her. James tended to favor a more settled existence, but he has no regrets as his travels provided such rich and exciting lives for him and his wife.

Eventually they moved back to South Florida where they discovered the beautiful area known as Port Charlotte, a small town on the west coast. To go at his own pace James opened a small real estate brokerage office staffed only by him and an elderly matron named Sally King. Port Charlotte had an abundance of prestige properties, many in beautiful waterfront settings. It was a community with the demographics that suited upper middle class families. The school systems were excellent, the town government was stable, and the building standards were high. There was no blight in this area. It was growing and enjoying a reputation for elegant Florida living. James' was not to be a typical real estate listing service. This was to be a boutique office where customers looking for upscale properties, a half million dollars and up, could come and James would find them what they were looking for in any of the nearby communities of Naples, Marco Island, or Ft. Meyers. He placed an ad in a real estate journal and the business started trickling in.

The seeds of James' trouble began when a certain customer named Osvaldo Sklar walked in his door and asked him to find some properties. He was looking to buy a number of upscale residential properties as investments. Sklar said he was a vice president of Lakeshore Bank in Coco Beach, with the responsibility of investing hundreds of millions of dollars of the bank's money. The part about being a vice president at Lakeshore was true. The part about investing hundreds of millions of dollars was never proven. James found Mr. Sklar a couple of residential properties, which he bought as investments. Mr. Sklar used Franklin Lee as his mortgage broker.

James had done a good job for Mr. Sklar. Happy with the results, Sklar introduced him to several other investors, including his two brothers, Rolando, a mortgage broker from Panama City, and Walter, a stockbroker from Dallas, Texas, and another officer of Lakeshore Bank named Elliott Wynn. James did a good job for these investors and, in the course of about seven months, ended up brokering fifteen properties to the investment group. But Osvaldo Sklar seemed upset, perhaps jealous of the other investors. They were able to buy multiple properties, and he could only qualify for two. Soon Sklar became a constant nuisance to James, always inquiring about the details of the transactions of the other investors. James refused to divulge any information as he felt he was in a fiduciary relationship with them. And the investors steadfastly refused to allow any of their information to be shared. At one point Osvaldo threatened James, telling him that he was going to call the FBI because he knew there was fraud committed during the loan process on the real estate deals he had brokered to his two brothers and Sean Dickens. James thought that Osvaldo was just venting, and responded that this was no concern to him because he was the real estate broker on the transactions and had no part in, or knowledge of the financing. By November of 2006 the fifteen real estate transactions had been closed. By appearances, with the exception of Osvaldo Sklar, all of the investors were satisfied with their purchases. James had acquired a reputation for being able to match properties to buyers' requirements. He was so busy being the consummate buyers' agent that he was turning business away.

In 2007 James received a visit from an FBI agent by the name of Wilson, who came to his office with no paperwork, and no warrants. He said he wanted to interview James about the transactions with Sklar and Wynn. Having nothing whatever to hide, James gave Wilson full access to his files. The files contained listing agreements, sales contracts, various correspondences related to the transactions, and closing documents. They contained no documentation related to the financing of the properties. Months later, on different occasions, some of the listing agents on the transactions contacted James to tell him that the FBI had been interviewing them and that he was under investigation.

On October 28, 2012, five years after Agent Wilson's first visit, six agents, two from FBI including agent Wilson, two from the U.S. Marshal's office, and two county sheriffs, all dressed in SWAT gear and ready for war, appeared at James' door. They used four SUVs to block the street outside

James' house. In a show of force more appropriate to the storming of a terrorist cell, they asked sixty-seven year old James to step outside. Wearing nothing but his pajamas, he cooperated. They slapped handcuffs on him and placed him under arrest. As they began to escort him away, James asked if they would permit him to get dressed. They agreed, and the six storm troopers entered the house and searched all the rooms and the garage. They were looking for guns and drugs, but there were none to be found.

At the same time they were about to cart James away in the back of the marshal's SUV, Maureen Watkins returned home with the family's two French Poodles in the car with her. She stopped the car and asked what was going on. As an officer approached, the dogs started barking wildly. Fearing that they may be shot, Maureen drove away. James and Maureen had by this time been together for fifty years. They had only each other, no children, and no close family. The separation that began at that traumatic moment lasted for more than three years.

James was taken to the Ft. Meyers courthouse where he appeared before the magistrate. He asked what this was all about. He knew of no charges or accusations. About half way through the hearing the prosecutor produced James's indictment. This was the first he had heard about it. Subsequent to the hearing, James was taken to the Lee County Jail and placed in a four-man cell. This was James's first night ever in jail.

On the following day things went horribly bad for James. He describes it as the worst day of his life, and one that he feels fortunate to have survived. In the courtroom James was trussed up with handcuffs, leg irons, and a restraining chain around his waist. His motion was very limited. He could not move his hands at all. While Assistant U.S. Attorney Crocker was discussing the charges, James' left handcuff snapped open. It had been improperly applied and slipped off. James was surrounded by marshals, four of them, no more than a few feet away. He turned to show one of his captors what had happened and was immediately seized upon and restrained further. The marshals, no doubt embarrassed by their failure to secure the prisoner properly, staged a dramatic seizure and re-cuffing of James. They were trying to make it appear that James had picked the lock on the handcuff. Very roughly the marshal manhandled him, shook him like a rag doll, and dragged him to a chair. (James's legs were in shackles so he could only take baby steps.) The marshal reattached the cuffs so tightly that the heavy metal bit into his wrist. In taking the side of the marshals, Judge Marcia Tripp railed that in her thirty years on the bench she had never seen such a brazen act in her courtroom. It was simply unacceptable that someone should attempt to escape from handcuffs right in front of her. It is impossible to believe that this was anything but theatrics on the part of the judge, but she followed it up with a draconian detention order.

At this point James was merely a suspect; he was not a criminal; he had not been convicted, and he openly declared his innocence. The charges, absurd as they were, were of a white collar, victimless nature. There was no threat to society, and James was not a dangerous man. Nor was he accused of such. But Judge Tripp's order not only rejected bond, but also ordered "the defendant be detained prior to trial and until the conclusion thereof." She further stated that "the defendant be committed to the custody of the Attorney General for confinement in a correction facility separate, to the extent practical, from persons awaiting or serving sentences, or being held in custody pending appeal." In plain English that meant throw sixty-seven year old James Watkins, with his aortic aneurism and other life threatening health issues, into solitary confinement until his trial.

From that hearing James was taken to a holding cell within the courthouse building. Here the marshal, angered and embarrassed at being exposed for improperly applying

166

the handcuffs that came off in front of an audience in the courtroom, had an opportunity to punish James in his own way. He placed two sets of handcuffs on James's wrists and tightened them down as far as they would go. Several chains were fastened around James's body so tightly that he could barely breathe. He was uncertain what kinds of restraints were holding his legs, but whatever it was had him limited to bending down in a crouching position. The bullying marshal said to him, "Let me see you get out of these chains." He simply could not move. In a matter of minutes James's hands swelled up to double their normal size and turned purple. He could only take shallow breaths because of the tight chain around his chest. His loose fitting prison pants had ridden down exposing his genitals and buttocks. His humiliation was complete, and his pain was unbearable. He screamed and screamed for help. His hands could take no more pressure - his thumbnails separated from their beds. Alert to his screaming, a marshal came by to see what the matter was. The marshal entered the cell and demanded that James get up onto the bench against the wall. James told him that he was bound too tight and could not move up to the bench. The marshal continued to insist that he get up on the bench. James again reiterated that he could not move, much less climb onto the bench. Finally, after nearly an hour of this torture, the marshal released the cuffs from James's right wrist. All James remembers is the feeling of the blood flow back into his arm, hearing his heart beat as the new blood rushed in, and later waking up. He had passed out from the strain on his heart caused by the sudden rush of blood out of his hand and arm.

Shortly after the trussing incident the marshal brought James his meal in a paper bag. James emptied the contents of the bag to find a black banana and a sandwich of the same color. When he peeled the banana he found it was crawling with maggots. He found the same thing when he unwrapped the sandwich. When he brought this to the attention of the marshal he was told, "We have special meals for prisoners like you. That's all we have for you, eat it or not, I don't care." At this point James had been charged with a single count of mail and wire fraud. It was only his second day in the system. He had not been tried, and he had not pled to a crime. Supposedly he was innocent until proven guilty. He was treated as if he had been declared guilty of a heinous crime and sentenced. Within a few days James filed a complaint to the internal affairs division of the U.S. Marshal's office in Washington, D.C. complaining of his torture within the walls of the federal courthouse. James later learned that an investigation had been conducted, but he never learned the outcome.

In compliance with the judge's confinement order, James was transported from the Federal Courthouse holding cell to the county prison. The prison had received the absurd advance notice that a prisoner was coming who had the ability to get out of handcuffs. When James shuffled out of the transport vehicle he was greeted by a number of sheriffs with shotguns at the ready. After the prison intake process he was placed in solitary confinement. During his month long stay in that jailhouse, James lived in his cell twenty-four hours a day. He was allowed ten minutes outside the cell three times a week. He could use this time to either shower or make a phone call. The showers did not have walls or a privacy curtain. They were behind a chain link fence. Female guards and other female staff would show up at shower time and watch James bathe. He had no privacy. It was degrading and humiliating.

James believes that the FBI investigation began with Osvaldo Sklar. Osvaldo had been acting strangely and irrational. He was threatening James and making a pest of himself. Agent Wilson told James that, from things he had learned from Sklar and his other investors, he could prove he was guilty of mortgage fraud, over-inflating property values, money laundering, and kickbacks. Wilson said that James was guilty of racketeering, and was part of the "mob". These accusations were profoundly absurd and would have been funny if they were not so serious.

But the case against James was very serious. Osvaldo Sklar, his brothers, Rolando and Walter, and Elliott Wynn had teamed up together to give testimony against James and Franklin Lee, the mortgage broker. They were given an Article Thirty-Five, meaning consideration in the way of reduced sentences would be given for their testimony against James Watkins and Franklin Lee. They had couched this case in such a way that made it look like James and Lee had conspired to commit mortgage fraud. Since mortgage fraud was the popular crime of the day, the FBI was happy to connect James, the successful real estate broker, with Lee, the successful mortgage broker. It was a tidy package for prosecutors, with the Sklars and Elliott Wynn willing to create facts that did not exist. Tying James to Franklin Lee hurt James' chances because Lee was the mortgage broker. Mortgage fraud was involved when the Sklar brothers and Elliott Wynn gave false income information on their mortgage applications. But James was not involved in the mortgage process, and had no way of knowing that the other parties had falsified their loan applications. James' involvement in the transactions was as real estate broker, and no real estate fraud had ever been alleged.

In his confinement order the judge recognized that James had a legitimate medical condition with his heart. He needed to be placed in a facility that had access to the special kind of care he needed. He was transferred to the Federal Detention Center (FDC) in Miami, which was only a few minutes from Jackson Memorial Hospital, the preferred health care provider in South Florida for the Bureau of Prisons.

James was placed in the SHU (Secure Housing Unit - solitary confinement) at FDC. Here he was in a cell by himself twenty-four hours a day. He was never allowed out of his cell. His meals were dropped through a hole in the cell door onto the filthy floor. James only ate the hard-boiled eggs and baked potatoes. These items could be eaten in a sanitary fashion unlike the rest of his meals that came in contact with the floor. During his grueling months in FDC Miami there were times when James had been shackled head to toe. He had been kept in solitary confinement, and he had nearly starved. He passed out twice and was taken to Jackson Memorial. His diagnosis was malnutrition.

James returned to the Collier County lockup for another appearance in court. This time he requested of the court to find him a new attorney. The public defender that had been selected for James had no experience in this kind of law. The judge agreed and granted his petition. A new attorney, a private one by the name of Ross Kelly, was appointed. Shortly thereafter Mr. Kelly visited James at Collier County. He handed James his business card. It read Ross Kelly, Criminal Defense Attorney. This pleased James, and he felt he was in good hands.

When James told his new attorney about the torture he had been through and the lies the FBI had made up, although sympathetic, Kelly told him to never say anything to the judge about this. The judge, the FBI, the prosecutor, and the marshals were all part of the same criminal justice system. The judge already did not like James, and complaining about the men who made up his "team" could only make things worse.

James was returned to solitary confinement at FDC Miami. Mr. Kelly visited several times. He seemed in favor of taking James's case to trial. Of course, James liked this plan as well. He had committed no crime, and he wanted the opportunity to prove his innocence in court. But then one day, several months later, the attorney came to visit saying, "I have good news for you." Naively James thought it was something like the charges had been dropped and he was going home. But that was not it. The prosecutor had offered a plea deal. If James would plead to wire and mail fraud he would recommend three years in prison, which would probably be reduced to two on account of James's health. James had one hour to accept the offer or the prosecutor would proceed with the trial and seek a prison term of eight to twenty years. James' thinking was: he could play Russian roulette, go to trial, and if he lost it would be like shooting himself in the head. Twenty years would be a life sentence. Or he could accept the plea offer and it would be more like shooting himself in the foot. At least someday he would be able to limp out of prison. He accepted the plea offer because he knew that the U.S. Attorneys won 97% of their cases. There was no level to which they would not stoop, including lying or producing false evidence, to maintain their winning record.

The plea and the sentencing took place in Federal Court in Miami. At sentencing the judge created an acrimonious climate. Attorney Kelly argued for a two-year sentence; the judge and the prosecutor wanted four years. There was no arguing; there was no discussion. Osvaldo Sklar and his brother, and Elliott Wynn, had all received five-year sentences (reduced to three for giving up James). The angry judge reasoned that if these men were serving three-year terms, then James, who he was now being referred to as the "ringleader", should have a longer sentence. When Kelly tried to argue that James had no part in the mortgage process, the judge was enraged. He shouted that it was within his power to impose an eight-year sentence if he wanted, and he would if the attorney didn't shut up. Mr. Kelly turned to James and said, "I can't say another word."

The judge sentenced James to forty-eight months in prison to be followed by three years of probation. He was ordered to pay $1,090,000 in restitution. He was then returned to FDC where he was placed in the general population for several months. After a year and a half

171

incarceration in Collier County and FDC Miami, James was shipped to the Federal Prison Camp at Pensacola, Florida, to finish the remainder of his sentence. Of his experience James says, "Up until this time I believed in the American way and its justice system. But I've learned that it is all lies. The Romans were called barbarians, but they did not shackle their un-convicted prisoners. The American system cannot be trusted. I live in fear because I have seen what they can do. I don't trust the government. Even if you maintain a low profile they can reach out and get you."

Of such behavior the great statesman, liberator, and famous ex-prisoner, Nelson Mandela once said, "It is said that no one truly knows a nation until one has been inside its jails. A nation should not be judged on how it treats its highest citizens, but its lowest ones."

From the White House to the Big House
The Scott Walker Story

The occasion was the dedication of the Bush Library on the campus of Southern Methodist University in Dallas, Texas. It was in the spring of 2014. The ex-President approached and spoke these words that Scott Walker will never forget, "Scott, I'm sorry for what's happening to you at this time. The current Justice Department is over-reaching." That telling comment from George W. Bush sums up a series of events that led to an investigation, a conviction, sentencing, and incarceration that never should have happened.

Scott Jared Walker was born on July 9, 1979 in Biloxi, Mississippi, the only child of Doctors William and Sharon Walker. William Walker's doctorate in toxicology was from Mississippi State University. For a dozen years, and under three different governors, he was the Executive Director of the Mississippi Department of Marine Resources (MDMR). In that position he managed a department with 300 employees and, in addition to his daily routine responsibilities, when the disasters of Hurricane Katrina in 2005 and the BP Oil Spill in 2010 hit the Mississippi Gulf Coast, Dr. Walker was the point man in the federal and state recovery efforts. Sharon Walker's doctorate in marine biology was from the University of Southern Mississippi. From 1980 until 2010 she was the Director of Education at the J.L Scott Marine Education Center and Aquarium in Biloxi. This facility was a beautifully conceived adjunct to the University of Southern Mississippi, but was unfortunately destroyed in 2005 by Hurricane Katrina. In 2010 Dr. Sharon Walker joined the Institute for Marine Mammal Studies (IMMS) as its director of education and outreach. IMMS was developing the new Ocean Expo, an ambitious aquarium project intended to be an educational center and rehab facility for marine mammals. As the son of two highly educated parents, it was inevitable that Scott would be exposed to excellent schooling, and raised in an environment that encouraged intellectual curiosity and personal achievement. This encouragement led to a career in government service that resulted in jobs as the personal assistant to one of the most powerful Senators in the history of the United States, and ultimately to a post in the West Wing of the White House.

Scott's interest in politics was peaked while earning his bachelor's degree in business administration at Ole Miss. He was an elected member of the Campus Senate each year, including his freshman year. Being able to influence policy appealed to Scott, so he decided to become a candidate for president of the student body in his senior year. The challenger was an African American student by the name of Nic Lott. Scott ran a vigorous campaign that resulted in a loss by eighty-one votes in a runoff, and Nic Lott became the first African American in the History of Ole Miss to occupy that office. The election, and Lott's victory, garnered national attention. Nic and Scott became close friends and even ended up as roommates while working as interns for Senator Trent Lott (no relation) in Washington, D.C.

It was Scott's close association with Senator Lott that helped to catapult him through the various offices of power in Washington. Trent Lott served as the U.S. Representative for the Southern District of Mississippi from 1972 until 1988. Following that office, Representative Lott was elected by the people of Mississippi to serve as one of its two United States Senators. He served four terms as Senator and rose to become the Senate Majority Leader. In that capacity he ran the Senate and held the third most powerful position in the country, on par with the Speaker of the House. Through his summer internship, between his junior and senior years in college, Scott became close friends with Trent Lott and his wife Tricia. He loved working for the Senator and considered taking time off from college to come to work full time. The Senator was quite fond of Scott as well, and told him to return to Ole Miss and get his degree, and after that he would hire him full time. As soon as Scott graduated, he returned to Washington to work for the Senator in the Senate Majority Leader's Office. He started in the mailroom but was quickly promoted with the title of Office Manager and Personal Aide. When Senator Lott accepted the post as Chairman of the Senate Rules and Administration Committee he appointed Scott to be his Executive Assistant.

Through his activities on behalf of the Republican Party, Scott was making friends with influential people on the state and national scenes. In 2003 an exciting opportunity was presented to Scott. Haley Barbour, the Governor-elect for Mississippi, called to tell him that he had submitted his name to Matthew Kirk, the Deputy Assistant to the President for Legislative Affairs. There was a job in that office, and Scott was the leading candidate. This was an exciting opportunity to go to work in the White House. Scott met with Senator Lott to tell him of the offer. But the Senator recommended that he remain with him in the Senate. Scott, ever the loyal team member, though disappointed, called Deputy Assistant Kirk and declined the offer. The following morning the Senator called Scott into his office. He told him that he and his wife had discussed the job offer and decided that it was in Scott's best interest to accept the job if it was still being offered. It was a once in a lifetime opportunity, and the Senator did not want to hold him back. Scott immediately called Kirk to see if the job was still available. He was told that if he wanted the job it was his. On that very same day Scott reported for work at the White House.

Scott's job was in the Office of Legislative Affairs - Senate, on the second floor of the West Wing. The broad definition of the function of this office was to lobby the

Senate on behalf of the President. Scott's title was Executive Assistant and Events Coordinator. Specifically Scott was to be present and facilitate meetings anytime a U.S. Senator met with the President. He helped with scheduling meetings and making certain that any Senator who had a meeting scheduled with President Bush would be greeted, escorted to the assigned meeting location, and available at the moment the President was ready. Anytime a Senator or group of Senators were with the President, whether it was in the White House, Camp David, in the presidential motorcade, on Air Force One, at bill signings, or at dinner in the private residence, Scott was there. He had the highest security clearance a White House staffer can have. He worked from 5 a.m. to 9 p.m. weekdays, and usually one day on the weekends. Scott figures he attended over 3,000 events while serving in that position. Few people in government worked closer to the President than Scott Walker did.

Although the work was at times exhausting, Scott knew that holding that position was a rare privilege. Not only did he perform the meet-and-greet and get to work closely with the President and many of the most powerful and famous people in the world, but he was also a witness to history on numerous occasions. Among his more memorable events, and people who impressed him, several stand out as particularly unforgettable.

• The first time Scott met Barak Obama, the latter was a junior Senator from the State of Illinois. President Bush was very cordial with Obama. He greeted him warmly and noted that they each had two daughters and strong wives. The President gave the Senator a personal tour of the State Dining Room, the Red Room, Green Room, Blue Room, and East Room. That same evening Scott was tasked with giving a personal tour of the entire West Wing to Michelle Obama and her two daughters, Sasha and Milea. He never dreamed that someday this family would occupy that office. Scott met with Obama many times after that event and enjoyed getting to know the future president.

• Swearing in ceremonies are always historical events. Scott staffed the swearings-in of such notable dignitaries as Supreme Court Justice Samuel Alito, Chief Justice John Roberts, Federal Reserve Chairman Ben Bernanke, all of the Cabinet members in George W. Bush's second term, and Senator John Danforth's swearing is as the U.S. Representative to the United Nations

• Scott also stood by as the President presented the nations highest military award, the Medal of Honor, to Tibor Rubin, for gallantry in action during the Korean conflict. Rubin was a corporal during that war and was finally awarded his medal at the age of seventy-six.

• Scott became acquainted with President Jimmy Carter through his efforts on behalf of Habitat for Humanity of Mississippi Gulf Coast in response to the Hurricane Katrina catastrophe. When asked to accompany him on a habitat build in Chang Mai, Thailand, and in Vietnam, Scott jumped at the opportunity. For two weeks Scott worked alongside President Carter and First Lady Rosalynn Carter building homes. Scott was impressed that President Carter actually jumped into the work, laying bricks and nailing lumber as they assisted in the building of 1,000 homes. Scott recalls, "I was very impressed with President Carter's energy, patience, and kindness. He is a unique individual and a true inspiration." Scott describes Jimmy Carter as one of the most sincere and genuinely fine men he met during his decade in federal government.

• Scott was present when Muhammad Ali received the Presidential Medal of Freedom from the President in the East Room of the White House. Ali was accompanied by his daughter, Laila, for the event. When Ali took the podium he spoke only a few words, "Thank you all, thank you to God." The gallery got to its feet for a standing ovation. There was not a dry eye in the house. Scott had his picture taken with

Ali in what appeared to be the boxer giving him a playful tap to the jaw. That photo is one of Scott's prize souvenirs from his time in government.

•   On the sad occasion of the Ronald Regan's funeral, while the President's body lay in State in the Capitol Rotunda, Nancy Regan was given a reception in the White House. Scott was tasked to escort Mrs. Regan from the First Lady's office in the East Wing to the Oval Office. During this ten minute walk Mrs. Regan spent the time reminiscing about her and her husband's days in the White House. While Mrs. Regan was talking about these better times, Scott was asking himself how he had ever gotten into such a position as to be accompanying this great and famous lady through the White House.

In the three years that Scott worked in the West Wing, he interacted with scores of famous and powerful people. Some of these he met with many times and got to know quite well. But when asked who impressed him the most, Scott's answer was a surprising one. He knew such personalities as Tom Hanks, Tom Brady, Jack Nicklaus, Lorne Michaels, Bono, Pope Benedict, Meg Ryan, Tiger Woods, Dennis Quaid, Vince Vaughn, and many others, any of whom would make for interesting stories. On the political side he met practically anybody who had influence including England's Tony Blair, Chicago Mayor Daley, Russian President Vladimir Putin, Germany's Angela Merkel. It was a daily occurrence to run into such powerful individuals as Donald Rumsfeld, Colin Powell, Vice President Dick Cheney, Condoleezza Rice, and most of the U.S. Senators and Representatives, as well as world leaders from every continent.

But it was Joey Bosik, a man of little renown, who impressed Scott as much as any. Bosik had suffered appalling injuries in the war in Iraq. Those injuries had left him a quadruple amputee. Bosik was in Walter Reed Hospital awaiting four prosthetic limbs when George Bush met him. Scott accompanied the President on that tour. Bosik told the President that all he wanted was to receive his new limbs so he could get back with his troops (that was never to happen.) The President was also impressed with Bosik and told him that when he received his artificial limbs he would be invited to the White House where the two could use the putting green to have some fun together. Scott monitored Bosik's progress, and when the time was right, the President followed through with the invitation. Senator Elizabeth Dole was present when Bosik showed up for his date with the President. Scott remembers, "The President was very cordial with Joey Bosik and his wife, Jamie. He liked him and was amazed by his spirit." Scott, too, was profoundly affected by his meetings with Bosik. "That was when the war became a reality for me," he says.

In the heady atmosphere of the West Wing, world-altering events happen everyday. Scott was witness to many of these events. Of particular note, Scott remembers the signing of the Katrina Relief Bill that authorized upwards of $100 billion for the restoration of the Gulf Coast. Scott accompanied President Bush for a tour of the devastated area only days after the hurricane. The devastation was overwhelming and a sight that Scott says he will never forget.

There are few greater honors than to be present at the signing of a major bill. Scott was present for dozens of bill signings. Of particular note was his attendance at the signing of the original Patriot Act and the Patriot Act of 2005. Also in attendance were such notable Washington heavyweights as Speaker Dennis Hastert, Representative Tom Delay, and Senators Bill Frist, Mike Enzi, and Ted Kennedy.

Also memorable was the annual breakfast in the White House for new Senators. Scott staffed several of those. He also staffed the Bipartisan Leadership Breakfast every two weeks where President Bush invited the Speaker of the House, Dennis Hastert, and House Minority Leader, Nancy

Pelosi, Senate Majority Leader Bill Frist, and Senate Minority Leader Harry Reid.

Not every person who Scott encountered in the White House left him with a positive impression. At a dinner at the Occidental Grill in the Willard Hotel, strongman Karl Rove said out loud to his dinner guests, "The easiest thing I ever did was to destroy Trent Lott." Rove knew of Scott's closeness to the Senator, and that the statement was intended to hurt him, and eventually get back to the Senator. "Karl Rove was a bully who sought revenge against anyone who got in his way," says Scott. The reference to the destruction of Senator Lott had to do with him losing his post as Majority Leader. On the occasion of the 100th birthday of Senator Strom Thurmond, in a toast given by Lott that was intended as an innocent compliment, Lott praised the elder statesman when he said, "When Strom ran for President in 1948, Mississippi voted for him. If the rest of the country would have followed our lead we would not have had all the problems we've had over all these years." Scott witnessed the bi-partisan crowd give a standing ovation in agreement with the Senator's statement. But once that statement was out, Rove went to work stirring up negative publicity for the Senator. In 1948 Senator Thurmond had run as a Dixiecrat, a movement that had a racial bias. This was not what Senator Lott had in mind when he made that toast. It was only intended to flatter the Senator. Rove called in the national media, and together they blew the story out of proportion. But this move by Rove accomplished its purpose. Senator Lott was tagged by the unfriendly press as a racist, a description that could not be further from the truth. But the damage was done, and with pressure from his Republican colleagues, Lott had to step down from his Majority post. Out of respect for all his good works over a lifetime of service, he was given the Chairmanship of the Senate Rules Committee by Senator Rick Santorum of Pennsylvania. Senator Lott was well known for being able to bring consensus in the Senate "across the aisle", meaning that he was expert at negotiating with Democratic Senators, which in turn helped the Senate to pass measures; to get things done. His effectiveness in working with the Republican Speaker of the House, Newt Gingrich, along with democratic President Bill Clinton, was epic. It will be remembered as one of the most effective combinations of opposing parties in the history of the country. Curiously, Rove, Lott, and Bush were all Republicans, and taking the Senator down was actually counter-productive to the Bush agenda.

In January of 2007 Senator Lott asked Scott to come back to work for him. In the intervening years the Senator had worked his way back up to become the Majority Whip, the second highest position in the Senate. He needed a good man to represent him in the Southern District of Mississippi, the Senator's home district, and the one he had represented when he was elected to the U.S. House of Representatives. In spite of the fact that George Bush had two more years to serve as President, and Scott was welcome to stay through the remainder of his term, a more fitting proposal came his way from Senator Lott. Funding was about to flow to the Mississippi Gulf Coast area after the devastation of Hurricane Katrina, and the Senator's district offices in Gulfport and Pascagoula needed someone he could rely upon to run them in his absence. The offer appealed to Scott. He had been away from his home for ten years and wanted to return to his family, and he desperately wanted to help the Mississippi Gulf Coast to recover. Scott accepted the job as the Southern District Field Representative. His job was to tend to the Senator's affairs while he was in Washington, and staffing the Senator when he was in the District. One year later Senator Lott retired. His successor was Senator Roger Wicker. Scott remained with Senator Wicker for eighteen months before embarking on a career outside the national spotlight.

In just a couple of years after Scott's return to Mississippi he had become a popular figure. He was an important part of the Hurricane Katrina relief effort through Senators Lott and Wicker's offices. In April 2009, with encouragement from friends, colleagues, and family he decided to run for public office, to try to become the Mayor of his hometown, Ocean Springs. At only twenty-nine years of age Scott launched a professional Republican primary campaign. Friends and other supporters held fund-raisers for Scott that were attended by such high profile individuals as Senator Lott, and Governors Haley Barbour and Phil Bryant. They raised over $200,000 for his campaign. His opponent in the primary was John McKay, a man who had served for thirty-five years in various public offices in Ocean Springs, and as president of the County Board of Supervisors. McKay knew everyone in the county; he was one of the 'good old boys'. Scott was now known as being instrumental in organizing the funding and the work associated with the Hurricane Katrina recovery, and for having powerful friends at the state and federal levels. He won the Republican primary handily against the long serving McKay. But in the general election Connie Moran, the incumbent, inched by Scott to win by eighty-eight votes out of 6,500 counted.

At the same time Scott was running for Mayor of Ocean Springs, his good friend Robbie Maxwell was running for the same office in Pascagoula, Mississippi. The two knew each other because Maxwell had been appointed Sergeant at Arms of the United States Senate during the same period that Scott was working for Senator Lott in his Washington office. Maxwell won his race and became the Mayor of Pascagoula. Already in operation at this time was the successful consulting firm Robert Maxwell and Associates. Maxwell already knew he could get along with Scott; they were best friends. He also knew that aligning himself with this popular figure could be good for business. The two men decided to join forces and opened Maxwell and Walker Consulting Group, LLC. Over time the new firm had more than fifty clients. As a lifestyle matter, neither wanted to spend eighteen hours a day working. Their priority was to spend quality time with their families, and act as a boutique lobbying firm. They limited their representation to ten clients at a time. This was the correct balance to allow them to do a superior job for their clients representing firms, such as construction and engineering companies, non-profit groups, and others who had dealings with the local, state, and federal governments.

The only time the firm ever represented a government entity, the City of D'Iberville, things went terribly wrong. It did not have to end up that way had it not been for an overly ambitious prosecutor and a few investigators who were willing to pressure witnesses into submission. The City had been trying for more than a year to secure a $3 million grant from the Governor's office to bring a raw water line from Back Bay Biloxi to the Ocean Expo site, a proposed $100 million aquarium and learning center. The City had made three appeals to Governor Barbour with no success. The Governor had control of a pool of BP relief funds under an act called the Gulf of Mexico Energy Security Act (GOMESA). These funds were to be administered by the Department of Marine Resources, Dr. Bill Walker's agency. But the City of D'Iberville could not make their proposal work, so they came to Maxwell Walker for help. The firm agreed to take the City on as a client.

The GOMESA funds were to be used at the digression of the Governor. Scott used his knowledge of the system, and close relationship with Governor Barbour and the governor's staff, to help get the project back on track. D'Iberville City Attorney, Dub Hornsby, was very motivated to get the project funded and he pushed the Maxwell Walker firm for results. The proper agency through which to funnel the funding might have been the Department of Marine

Resources, but Hornsby had specific preferences for how he wanted the funding to take place. For one thing, the City Mayor, Rusty Quave, worked for the MDMR as a low-level field worker. For another, because Scott's father was the head of MDMR, Hornsby wanted to avoid the appearance of impropriety with Maxwell Walker in contract with the city for a consulting fee. Scott and Robbie made the request to Governor Barbour and received his approval. It was arranged that the funding would go through another state agency, the Department of Environmental Quality (DEQ).

On March 19, 2011 the Maxwell Walker Consulting Group's private single engine Cherokee took off from the Ocean Springs airport with Scott and two friends, Dax Pitalo and Trey O'Bryant, and a hired pilot. Scott was returning from the Boy's and Girl's Club Charity Golf Tournament, which he had sponsored, and the trio were headed to Destin, Florida. They were to be dinner guests of Gregg Drescher, a friend who Scott frequently called on to support local and statewide candidates. It was a very warm day, the plane was overloaded, and the Ocean Springs runway was a short one. Upon rotation it appeared questionable that the airplane had enough speed and lift to clear the trees at the end of the runway. In an attempt to gain altitude the pilot pointed the nose of the plane at an impossibly steep angle. Overweight and too slow for this maneuver, the plane lost lift, stalled, and crashed. There were no fatalities, but there were limbs broken and many other cuts and bruises. Scott's injuries were the most severe. He was rushed to the Singing River Hospital where it was discovered that his vertebral disjointment had come within one millimeter of severing his spine. He was rushed into a six-hour surgery followed by a full body cast to stabilize his movements. Two days later he was taken by ambulance to the Methodist Rehabilitation Center in Jackson, Mississippi. Over time he learned that the initial surgery had not gone well, and his back would need to be re-broken and a different surgery performed.

In December of 2011 the Governor signed off on the Ocean Expo raw water line project. The $3 million grant was funded, and the money was placed in the City of D'Iberville's general fund. Maxwell Walker was paid its 6% ($180,000) fee pursuant to a unanimous approval from the City Council. Several years later in an audit by the DEQ it was learned City Attorney Dub Hornsby paid himself a fee in excess of $400,000 that he said the City owed him for services. Much of the rest of the $3 million was used for general obligations of the City. In that same audit that revealed the discovery of the Hornsby fee, it was learned that about half the GOMESA grant to the City of D'Iberville had been spent on projects other than Ocean Expo raw water line. In the end, Ocean Expo never got off the ground. DEQ took back what remaining funds there were from the grant, and ultimately Dub Hornsby became the subject of an FBI investigation for this and other matters involving the City of D'Iberville.

Between 2010 and 2012 Dr. William Walker was subjected to unwarranted scrutiny in the press. As the point man in the allocation of BP oil spill recovery funds for the Mississippi Gulf Coast, no matter how diligently he tried to be fair and direct funds to their intended uses, the press found fault at every turn. Months of bad press brought extraordinary pressure and ultimately led to a state audit and FBI investigation. And, while Scott had dealings with the State, and even with the MDMR, no negotiation between him and any of the agencies of which his father was an employee, member, or director were ever found to be inappropriate. Case in point, when Scott offered land he owned to be sold to the Mississippi Land Trust, an organization that purchases land for blue ways development, neighborhood parks, bird watching areas, and the preservation of natural areas, his application to the State to consider the purchase was found in order. The land was exactly the kind of site for which the Trust was founded. Land Trust Director Judy Stecker, and MDMR employee, Tina Shumate, helped walk Scott through the bureaucratic steps necessary to qualify his property for purchase. Neither Scott not his father profited from the sale of the land.

In the days when Scott worked for Senators Lott and Wicker, the use of the Senators' office to advance the agenda of the MDMR, where Dr. Walker was its Executive Director, were treated as a novelty by the media. That the son of the Director might be in a position to benefit the state was uplifting press, and the father and son were media darlings. The State of Mississippi, and the MDMR, benefitted greatly on account of this unique situation. But, when Scott resigned from his position with Senator Wicker to run for Mayor of Ocean Springs, and become a lobbyist with Robbie Maxwell, the press repeatedly tried to make his relationship with the state appear unseemly. When the press started criticizing him, with no proof or evidence of wrongdoing, only accusations with no basis in fact, long time friends and public figures turned against him, lied about him, and failed to come to his defense. Among the names of men who Scott never would have believed would turn on him were Haley Barbour, the Governor who had earlier recommended Scott for the White House job; Robbie Maxwell, his best friend, business partner, and the man for whom Scott named his son, Max; Bob Byrd, Scott's godfather and a family friend for forty years; and Dub Hornsby, the City Attorney for D'Iberville, and the man who pushed Scott the hardest for the Ocean Expo grant, and walked away from the failed aquarium project with nearly a half million dollars.

In 2004 Governor Barbour tasked Dr. Walker with starting the Mississippi Department of Marine Resources Foundation. Funding that went into the Foundation was earmarked for the Rigs to Reefs Program which converted older, closed oil rigs into habitats for fish stocks. In support of its purpose the Foundation leased two boats from the YMCA. One of those leases was prepared by Attorney Joseph Runnels of the State's Attorney General's Office, the other was prepared by the Walker family friend, Bob Byrd. During its existence the Foundation entertained officials from state and federal offices, U.S. Senators, oil executives, wealthy contributors, and Federal Judges. The Foundation raised over $10 million for the reefs project. But later investigators and the press would try to make this excellent program look like it had committed a crime.

On account of the negative press and complaints against the MDMR, mainly from disgruntled contractors who were unable to qualify for contracts related to the BP cleanup, the State decided to look into the allegation that state funds had been misspent on the Rigs to Reefs project. On October 28, 2012 examiners from State Auditor Stacey Pickering's office appeared at the MDMR headquarters. They were armed with warrants, and accompanied by FBI agents with badges flashed and weapons drawn. The press had been tipped off and a media crowd was outside with TV trucks and reporters waiting for a story. Dr. Walker was humiliated when he was made to wait in a holding room outside the Executive Director's office while investigators confiscated files and hard drives. It appeared that no matter how innocent he may have been in reality, Dr. Walker's fifty-year career in public service was in jeopardy. The press had been attacking him and Scott unmercifully. The Sun Herald, the Mississippi Gulf Coast's main newspaper, and the one that had named Dr. Walker one of the ten most influential businessmen on the Gulf Coast over forty years of age, and had named Scott one of the ten most influential businessmen on the Gulf Coast under forty years of age, took a turn and vehemently went after the Walker family. They sensationalized the story of the Walkers in more than 200 articles.

During this time William Walker was in Miami, on personal leave from the MDMR. Scott had been flown there to the University of Miami, Jackson Memorial Hospital for his corrective back surgery. The father and son had set up household in a condo on Brickell Avenue while Scott underwent a second surgery and rehabilitation. The professional world of the Walker family was crumbling. As busy as Dr. Walker was at this time, doing everything he could to care for his son, when the Commissioner of Marine Resources suspended him without pay at the direction of the Governor, he felt a responsibility to return to Mississippi to fight these allegations, and try to rescue his career. He chartered a medical Citation jet and returned home with his son.

Early on, Robbie Maxwell and Scott Walker determined that in order to be effective lobbyists they would have to be politically active. They supported candidates, held fundraisers, and routinely were asked by civilians and politicians for favors, and to use their influence to promote agendas. Scott's elegant beachfront home on the Mississippi Gulf Coast in Ocean Springs was the site of many political and social events. In October of 2012, just two weeks prior to the raid on MDMR headquarters, Scott held a fundraiser for Governor Mitt Romney's Presidential campaign. Present at the event were 400 guests including Governor Romney, his son, Josh Romney, U.S. Congressman Steven Palazzo, and many statewide Republican supporters.

Also present were a few undercover investigators who Scott did not know or recognize, and who would later prove to be profoundly damaging to Scott's future. "When the government sends agents to come spy on a political rally of a legitimate candidate for a high public office, there's something wrong about that," says Scott. "It's 'big brother' sticking his nose where it doesn't belong. No one is safe from a police force that has no check on its authority and no accountability to the public it is supposed to be protecting." Political observers believe that it was no coincidence that the raid on MDMR headquarters was timed just following the Romney fundraiser.

In another stroke of bad timing, Scott's wedding to his lovely fiancée, Trinity Ryals, was set to be held at his home on November 3, just five days after the MDMR raid. The date had been set far in advance, and preparations for the big event had been in the making for months. Five hundred of the Who's Who of Mississippi gentry had confirmed their attendance. Minutes after the news of the MDMR raid, the cancellations started coming in. Two hundred invitees, including the Governor, had backed out.

Four months after the Romney fundraiser, Scott logged on to his home security system from his office in Gulfport and saw that his house was surrounded by state auditors, FBI agents, and the press. The agents had been trying to call Scott on his cell phone and left several messages. On advice of his attorney Scott neither took the call, called them back, or returned home to admit them. Scott watched on his surveillance monitor as the ten agents knocked down his front door. The media stood by outside for three hours while the agents trashed the house. Furniture was overturned, holes were punched in the walls, Scott's prized picture of himself with President Bush and Vice President Cheney was broken and, on an embarrassing note, Trinity's underwear drawer was emptied out on their bed. A receipt of items confiscated was left evidencing the taking of a home computer, an expensive camera, various music CDs, cell phones, and computer thumb drives. Something they took that they did not itemize, or admit to, was a picture of Scott with the Mississippi State Auditor, Stacey Pickering.

In the ensuing months, state and federal investigators worked to craft cases against William and Scott Walker. They wanted to show the grant from the DEQ to the City of D'Iberville as tainted. Their cases made a great deal of noise about the operation of the MDMR, and particularly the Mississippi Land Trust and its purchase of Scott's property. With respect to the governor's authorization of GOMESA funds for the D'Iberville Ocean Expo project, investigators were out to prove that Maxwell Walker did nothing to earn their fee, and that the entire transaction was designed as a kickback scheme among insiders working with a state agency. While both transactions were legitimate, and stood up to exhaustive scrutiny, FBI agents and AUSA John Dowdy were able to intimidate key witnesses to build cases against the Walkers.

Scott and William Walker were ordered to appear at the FBI office in Gulfport at 9:00 a.m. on November 7, 2013, along with three co-defendants: Michael Janus, the City Manager of D'Iberville, and a business partner of Scott's in a venture called JAWA Investments, LLC (Janus Walker); Tina Shumate, the Director of the Coastal Planning Division of the MDMR; and Joe Ziegler, the Chief of Staff of the MDMR. Charges against Scott, his father, and Tina Shumate were related to the sale of Scott's property to the Mississippi Land Trust. Charges were also filed against Scott and Michael Janus related to the $3 million grant for the Ocean Expo raw water pipeline project.

This was the day for the FBI to put on a show for the press. All of the defendants were shackled by hands and feet and taken to the courthouse in Gulfport. While other defendants were taken by inside passage to the waiting vans, Scott was made to march outside into an alleyway where the press was crowded around for a paparazzi photo op. They got what they came for, and Scott's picture in shackles appeared on the front pages of the next day's newspapers.

Following the reading of the charges in court, and the setting of bond, the defendants were set free. Again the press was waiting to get more pictures and hoping for a comment. Scott's attorney, the very capable and iconic Arthur Madden, refused to allow Scott to address the press, so the media was able to say and print whatever it wanted with no rebuttal. It was an ugly time punctuated by fear, heartbreak, and abandonment. But Arthur Madden knew how the federal criminal justice system and public opinion could sway things. Negotiations between Madden and prosecutor Dowdy commenced. The prosecution was only looking for a public conviction. It really wasn't interested in punishing Scott with years of imprisonment and heavy fines. Arthur Madden did wonders on Scott's behalf. The prosecutors were willing to negotiate a plea bargain that would have resulted in a possible six-month sentence, but they would actually seek no jail time, and home confinement or probation, if Scott would plead guilty to a single count of federal program fraud involving the D'Iberville grant. Scott remembers sitting in Henrietta's Cafe in downtown Ocean Springs as his attorney practically begged him to take the deal. Madden knew what he was talking about, and he knew it was the right move.

Scott saw it differently. He knew that he had done nothing wrong, and that Governor Haley Barbour would testify that he had authorized the grant, and that Maxwell Walker had earned the fee. He thought Robbie Maxwell, Bob Byrd, and Dub Hornsby, who all knew the truth, and would come forward to testify for him. He was also thinking about his future. He loved public service; he loved doing great things for people as he had in the Katrina Relief project, and so many other events in the Trent Lott Senate office, and the Bush White House. A federal conviction would end any possibility of involvement like that again in the future. He was determined to fight the charges and clear his name.

In the case of the United States of America versus Scott Walker, the prosecution contended that the $3 million grant to the City of D'Iberville was intended as a kickback scheme so that Maxwell Walker could collect a fee for doing nothing. Michael Janus was the non-voting City Manager of D'Iberville, and a partner of Scott's in the JAWA venture. JAWA was an operating company that owned a number of investments including a condo in Oxford, Mississippi, a restaurant and bar in Biloxi called The Columns, and several boats that were leased out for the BP oil spill recovery effort. Shortly after the funding of the $3 million grant and the payment of the $180,000 fee to Maxwell Walker, Robbie and Scott agreed to lend the JAWA venture $90,000. Maxwell Walker frequently made investments and loaned money out, and the JAWA loan was quite typical. Loan documents were drawn by Scott's lifelong friend and godfather, Bob Byrd. JAWA immediately began making regularly scheduled payments under the note to Maxwell Walker. A total of $12,000 on the loan was paid back prior to any indictments. The prosecution characterized this loan transaction as a scheme to kickback money to Michael Janus.

On the allegation that the loan to JAWA was tainted, Scott thought he could call on Bob Byrd to testify that it was a legitimate loan transaction. On the allegation that Maxwell Walker did nothing to earn the fee, Scott thought he had Haley Barbour, who was the governor who authorized the grant, to vouch for him. Haley Barbour was a friend of Scott for years. It was Haley Barbour who recommended Scott for his White House job. It was Haley Barbour who stopped by Scott's office on his frequent trips to the White House. Governor Barbour toured the Katrina devastated Gulf Coast with Scott and Senator Thad Cochran. For years Scott was close friends with, and attended the wedding of Barbour's son, Reeves, in the governor's mansion. It was Haley Barbour who tried to hire Scott to be the Director of his Office of Gulf Coast Recovery when Senator Lott retired in 2008. Over the course of the dozen or so years that Haley Barbour was a friend of Scott and the Maxwell Walker firm, he always knew he could rely on them to support his causes through his political action committee called Haley PAC. Scott and Maxwell Walker contributed, and raised hundreds of thousands of dollars for Haley Barbour sponsored causes. Scott believed that he could surely rely on his friend to simply tell the truth about Maxwell Walker's involvement in securing the GOMESA grant for D'Iberville, and help make this nightmare go away.

In the matter of the United States of America versus William Walker, centered around the sale of land to the Mississippi Land Trust, although Dr. Walker was not an owner of the property, and the land met all of the criteria according to the mission statement of the Trust, Prosecutor Dowdy argued that because Dr. Walker had co-signed the note on the property for his son, that he was unjustly enriched by the sale. It might have been understandable that the prosecutor would have gone after Dr. Walker if he were a habitual offender who routinely abused his position as head of the MDMR, and had actually done something illegal. But Dr. Walker was the right man for the top job at MDMR. He accomplished great things for the State of Mississippi and the Gulf Coast. He handled the Katrina relief effort and the BP oil spill. He brought millions of dollars into the state. He served under three governors, and no man would say that he was anything but hard working, competent, and honorable. To be charged in the matter of the Land Trust purchase is a disgrace on the Grand Jury, the prosecutor, and the court. But Dr. Walker had an excellent team of attorneys in Bill Kirksey, Robert Walker, and Jan Baron. They knew that winning at trial in federal court was nearly impossible. It is rarely done, and the consequences of losing can be horrible. As a plea bargain, Attorney Dowdy offered a five-year term in federal prison if Dr. Walker would plead to a single count of conspiracy. Should he not accept the plea, Dowdy would charge him on five separate counts and seek a ten-year sentence, which at sixty-nine years of age, is practically a life sentence. Sadly, Dr. Walker was forced to take the plea offer, and was subsequently convicted and sent to the federal prison at Oakdale, Louisiana.

As instructed by Scott, Arthur Madden turned down the initial plea offer and started making calls to Haley Barbour for assurance that he would tell the truth and stick up for Scott. They were looking for Barbour to say that he had authorized the GOMESA grant, and that Maxwell

Walker had made the deal happen, and had earned the fee. When Barbour went silent and could not be reached by Madden, or Scott, or others who were trying to get his attention on Scott's behalf, they approached Victor Mavar, a long time friend and Barbour's biggest supporter on the Mississippi Gulf Coast. Mavar made the call and got through. Barbour told him that he had received the calls, emails, and fed ex letters, but he didn't want to get involved. In that conversation he admitted that Maxwell Walker had gotten the D'Iberville deal done and had earned the fee. The matter was very ugly in the press, and Haley Barbour was part of a very successful lobbying firm, Barbour, Griffith, and Rodgers in Washington, and had just joined the law firm of Butler Snow in Jackson, Mississippi. He didn't want to jeopardize potential massive earnings, even if it meant a close friend and supporter with a young family and brilliant career would go to federal prison.

Without Barbour's support the defense team's odds of success were diminished to near zero. Disappointed, deflated, and terrified, Scott instructed Arthur Madden to go back to the prosecutor to see about another plea offer. Upon doing so he was informed that the original plea offer was off the table, and a new arrangement would have to be structured. Instead of pleading to a single count in the D'Iberville/Ocean Expo matter, Scott would be required to also plead guilty in the Land Trust case as a co-defendant with his father. The prosecution would seek two eighteen-month sentences to run concurrently. He was no longer being offered home confinement and/or probation.

In order to convince Madden and his client of the wisdom of accepting the offer, the prosecution supplied copies of the 302s of Robbie Maxwell, Bob Byrd, and Dub Hornsby. The 302 Procedure is the record of interviews with potential witnesses. To say potential witnesses is a bit of a misnomer, because from testimony in the 302s, it was obvious that Maxwell, Byrd, and Hornsby were reciting

194

exactly what the prosecution wanted to hear to slam Scott. They were at least coerced; probably coached as well. Robbie Maxwell, Scott's closest friend going back to their early days working in the U.S. Senate in Washington, and now business partner, testified that the deals done between the MDMR and Maxwell Walker were done more on account of the father/son relationship between William and Scott than on their merits alone. Scott found that statement to be odd as it was Robbie Maxwell who had all the contact with the MDMR staff. In Bob Byrd's 302 he said that he felt the loan to JAWA was an improper kickback to Michael Janus. That too was a curious statement, as it was Byrd who drafted the loan documents, who closed the loan, and who knew that the regularly scheduled principal and interest payments were being made by Michael Janus and Scott. In 2013 Dub Hornsby told the FBI that he had never seen the contract between the City of D'Iberville and Maxwell Walker Consulting Group. In reality, it was Hornsby who prepared the agreement and instructed Michael Janus and Scott Walker on how and when to sign the contract. Hornsby had submitted the 2012 2nd Quarter Report from the City of D'Iberville to DEQ. That report included the contract between the City and Maxwell Walker. This was the physical evidence that he had seen the contract prior to the FBI interview in 2013. That contract was the basis upon which the City voted to pay Maxwell Walker its fee.

So, in the end, four men who Scott had always thought had been friends and could be relied upon to protect and defend him, let him down in the worst possible way. Haley Barbour, who could not repay Scott's loyalty and friendship in a hundred lifetimes, refused to get involved. Hopefully the fortune he is earning by not getting muddied in the Scott Walker case, even though he was part of it from the beginning, will help him sleep at night. And as to the best friend and business partner, Robbie Maxwell, one has to wonder how the prosecutor was able to get him to bend the truth. Perhaps to avoid being indicted himself? After all, Robbie received the same amount of money as Scott for the work done on the D'Iberville grant. And Bob Byrd, family friend, next door neighbor, and godfather, a man who had been nominated for a federal judgeship and was a well recognized citizen of Southern Mississippi; what pressure did he have hoisted upon him to make such damaging statements as to send an innocent man, his godson, to prison? Dub Hornsby, the D'Iberville City Attorney could have, and should have, admitted to his knowledge of the contract between the City and Maxwell Walker. After all, it was he who drafted it in the first place. But, facing troubles of his own with federal investigators, perhaps he thought it sounded better to deny knowledge of the arrangement, even in the face of having taken a large portion of the grant money himself. And Tina Shumate had a hand in this as well. It was Ms. Shumate who helped guide and structure the purchase of Scott's land to the Mississippi Land Trust. And it was also Ms. Shumate whose charges were dropped the day following William and Scott Walker's guilty pleas in court. What a curious stroke of timing that as soon as Dr. Walker and Scott were declared guilty, Ms. Shumate's legal problems with the feds went away. One has to wonder what information, true or false, she provided to the prosecution to receive such favorable treatment.

Scott is philosophical about the events that led to his incarceration. He and his father were both railroaded by a criminal justice system that mistakes punishment for justice. Injustice is what happened to him and his family. "Prison for me has been the separation from my two young boys, my wife, and my parents. I can endure the lockdowns, the brutality of life in a federal prison camp. What I cannot endure is the burden this experience has placed on my wife and my mother, and my helplessness to do anything about it." Sharon Walker was in her later 60s when her two men were taken from her. Retired after forty years of public service, and planning to spend her sunset years enjoying the family she spent a lifetime nurturing, she has been left alone to do what she can to help Trinity, and to worry about William and Scott. And what about Trinity? Her future plans were put on hold. She was going to be half the team that would raise her babies, help manage the family and household, along with Scott, who was already on a path to the stars. All that changed, casting her into the role of head of the family with responsibilities greater than she ever imagined. It is easy to sympathize and empathize with these two steel magnolias whose lives were taken away, and who were left to do the heavy lifting on account of a terrible miscarriage of justice.

White collar criminals, physicians, scientists, bankers, home builders, educators, judges, hospital administrators, some of the most highly educated and productive people in the world, languish in federal prison camps, their talents being wasted, while the ones at home are being left to suffer alone. It is a badly broken criminal justice system that makes innocent people suffer while the Justice Department sits idly by repeating its mistakes day in, day out, year in and year out, with no concrete agenda for ending the waste and pain.

Scott Walker self-surrendered to the Federal Prison Camp at Pensacola, Florida, on December 1, 2014 to begin serving his sentence. Being labeled a felon will place limits on his choices for future activities. It may slow him down, but it will not stop him. He is determined to continue working in service to fellow Mississippians, but much more important to him is the greatest lesson of all. "Prison has taught me to slow down and discover what is most important. Family is the most important thing. I am blessed with loving parents, a wonderful wife, and two beautiful sons. They need me, and I need them. I will remember this lesson in values for the rest of my life, and I will be thankful that I have this second chance to be a better son, husband, and father."

Epilogue

The amount of pain inmates endure, both those who are innocent and those who are guilty of crimes, is difficult to fathom. Consider what it must be like for a man or woman who has young children who are two, four, and six years old, who is sentenced to fifteen years in prison. That family's life becomes an epic struggle. What may have had a chance to be a normal, functioning, tax paying family is torn to shreds. A parent, breadwinner, role model, source of comfort, will no longer be there to watch and help his/her children grow up. This world is difficult enough for the two-parent, two-income household to grow and prosper. It is exponentially more difficult for the single parent with a spouse behind bars to provide the life the children need.

Admittedly, there are thousands of felons who sit in prisons for all the right reasons. The prisons are full of criminals who are where they belong. Society is safer because these men and women are locked away. Some have created crimes so heinous that they should never be set free. The streets are also full of people like that. Some people are just plain evil, and the criminal justice system helps to protect us from them. For this we are all grateful.

I have witnessed the pain an inmate feels as his wife and young children leave the prison visitation room on a Sunday afternoon, knowing they might not be back for several weeks or months, or ever. I experienced it myself. And I was one of the lucky ones who had frequent visits from my wife, children, grandchild, and friends. Such events are what helped us make it through. But I also knew many people who had very infrequent visits from their families, and some who had no visits at all. The heartbreak is unbearable to experience, and to witness. I know men whose wives waited for six or eight years, but could wait no longer, and broke off the marriage. The inmates, their families, and others who are affected by it experience every imaginable emotion.

A complaint that is voiced most often by inmates and their families centers on minimum mandatory sentencing. If a felon has a certain number of points, or is convicted of trafficking in various quantities of different classes of narcotics, there are guidelines by which the judge must abide in the sentencing. Sometimes the judges would like to go easy on a person for any number of reasons. First time offenders, white-collar criminals, highly trained professionals, and the list goes on. Their productivity, which contributes to the welfare of our communities, is cut off, usually permanently. What if that individual is named as a co-conspirator, in which case his degree of participation in the crime is at question? When it comes to sentencing, which is the job of the judge, the MM guidelines dictate its length. Even if the judge has heard testimony that makes him want to mitigate the sentence, he does not have that power. The sentence is arbitrary and impersonal. The judge's power to judge is diminished, and the convict is now the victim. And the family and community suffer for this.

Most of my prison friends in this story have been released, but not before suffering greatly from injustices that were hoisted upon them and their families. Several other stories I wrote that were just as compelling as these; some more so, were not included. The inmates that are the subject of those stories preferred to not have them published because their cases are on appeal. We don't want to fuel the anger of their accusers or judges. These individuals already have enough trouble.

Could there be a positive takeaway from all this? Rarely. Perhaps the inmate who is safer in prison than he would be in the streets is better off. Some inmates work on their education; some earn high school diplomas, or college degrees. Some convicts who had no marketable skills before incarceration learn a trade, but that's fairly rare. It is much more common for an inmate to waste away in a cell, or to learn some new tricks on how to commit bigger crimes.

Nearly everyday we see on the news a story about a cop who overreacts to a situation and a "perpetrator" gets beaten up, kicked, or killed. In those instances it takes some egregious behavior, usually accompanied by video evidence, for the victim to receive relief. The law is on the side of the police, prosecutors, and for the most part, politicians. And many of these police, prosecutors, and politicians are thoroughly corrupt, and are themselves a danger to society.

I am an advocate for criminal justice reform, and I am the first person to admit that defense attorneys and their clients make stuff up in their defense that is complete BS. There is abuse on both sides of the law. My sentiments lean toward true justice whereby an accused person must be given a chance to stage a reasonable defense; where the system must prove guilt.

So, let me tell of an incident that might help to highlight a point: I was invited on a fishing trip on the boat of a friend of a friend. The friend who invited me prepared me for what was about to come. My friend is an insurance executive for a well-known company. He even told me that he would have liked to correspond with me while I was in prison but was concerned that if the home office heard about it, he might have some explaining to do. I told him I understood. The fellow who owned the boat we were going out on was also an agent for the same company. And the other guest on the boat was a friend of the boat owner, and a retired circuit court judge. My friend's request of me was that I not say anything about my criminal past, to keep it on the down low. Some people might take offense at this, but I fully understand, and am too respectful to do otherwise. I appreciate a day of fishing, and know how to keep my mouth shut. So, introductions were made all around, and we cast off for the deep blue. The fishing was pretty good. It kept us busy and our spirits were high.

I can't remember a time in my life before this where there was an opportunity for me to have an open conversation with a judge. And this guy was no new judge. In fact he had just retired from the bench after more than two decades. He was very experienced. He had a lifetime of family court, civil cases, and criminal law. I was so intrigued by his background that I had to ask about his experiences. He had certainly seen it all. I asked if he had seen much abuse of the system from prosecutors or investigators. His response was that he had witnessed none of that, or very little of it, but he had seen much of the opposite, abuse of the system from lying and cheating defense attorneys and their clients. That made perfect sense to me. We became engrossed in the conversation, and I believe he enjoyed my intelligent curiosity, and probably appreciated the opportunity to revisit his past. He volunteered a lot of insight he had acquired over the years. It was great fun talking to him, a real eye opener. Then he said something that really captured my attention. He said words to the effect, "If I ever had to run for the office of public defender, I probably would not get elected. My motto would be, 'We'll give you a fair defense, and then throw your ass in jail where it belongs.'" How's that for a fair and balanced approach to justice by a respected career jurist?